Galatians 5:13-15, For you, my brothers and sisters, were called to freedom; only do not let your freedom become an opportunity for the sinful nature (worldliness, selfishness), but through love serve and seek the best for each other. For the whole Law [concerning human relationships] is fulfilled in one precept, "You shall love your neighbor as yourself [that is, you shall have an unselfish concern for others and do things for their benefit]." But if you bite and devour each other, watch out or you will be destroyed by each other.

Micah 6:6-8, With what shall I come before the Lord [to honor Him] and bow myself before God on high? Shall I come before Him with burnt offerings, with yearling calves? Will the Lord be delighted with thousands of rams, or with ten thousand rivers of oil? Shall I present my firstborn for my acts of rebellion, the fruit of my body for the sin of my soul? He has told you, O man, what is good; And what does the Lord require of you except to be just, and to love [and to diligently practice] kindness (compassion), and to walk humbly with your God [setting aside any overblown sense of importance or self-righteousness]?

Copyright © 2023 by Sylvester Antley Clark
All rights reserved.
No part of this book may be reproduced in any manner without the prior written permission from the publisher, except for the use of brief quotations in reviews and scholarly work.
For permissions or bulk sales, use the website below.

ISBN 979-8-3961-4121-6

First Published by URMIA in 2023

UNIVERSAL RESTORATION MINISTRY IN ACTION
UniversalRestorationMinistryInAction.org

Biblical passages cited in this book were taken from THE HOLY BIBLE, NEW INTERNATIONAL VERSION®, NIV® Copyright © 1973, 1978, 1984, 2011 by Biblica, Inc.® Used by permission. All rights reserved worldwide.

CHOOSE THIS DAY!

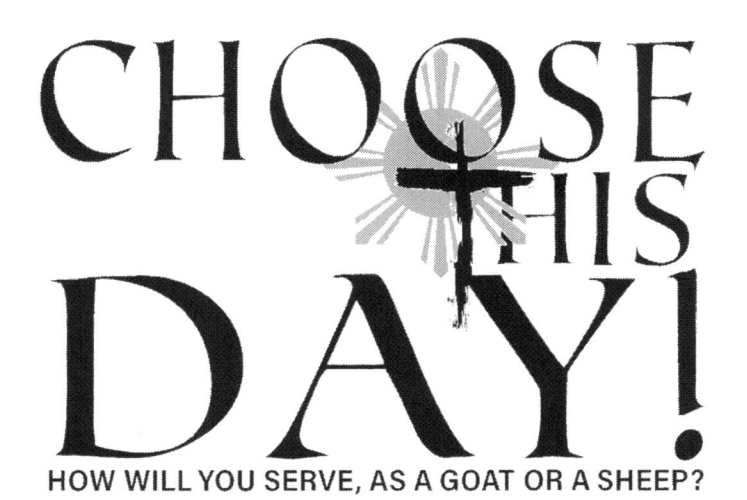

HOW WILL YOU SERVE, AS A GOAT OR A SHEEP?

SA CLARK

Contents

Introduction   vii

CHAPTER 1   1
Everything You Ever Wanted to Know About Sheep

CHAPTER 2   5
The Story of Abraham

CHAPTER 3   37
The Sheep and the Goats

CHAPTER 4   77
The Declaration of Independence and the US Constitution

CHAPTER 5   121
The Way Toward Freedom

CHAPTER 6   135
Save the Rams

CHAPTER 6   163
Conclusion

References   169
About the Author   175

Introduction

There is a familiar passage of scripture, Matthew 10:16, that is greatly misunderstood. Jesus is sending The Apostles out on their first evangelistic mission and He tells them, "I am sending you out as sheep among wolves." A major part of the misunderstanding comes from the fact that these were grown men, despite referring to them as lambs. Jesus wasn't sending out lambs, He was sending out rams (adult male sheep), and rams aren't weak nor passive.

Until God put it in my heart to write this book, I didn't know that rams were sheep. I always thought sheep are what is depicted in all the books, television shows, and movies I've seen. But now I know that what was depicted were ewes (adult female sheep) and lambs (sheep under one year old).

Rams can fight. Rams are tough, fierce, and tenacious. Trucks are named after rams. As a matter of fact, when God was compelling me to write this book the Los Angeles Rams (NFL football team) were in the playoffs, and I said, Lord, if the Rams make it to the Super Bowl and win that'll be my confirmation that you want me to write this book.

The initial title I had for this book was "Where are the Rams?" But the title had to change because God took me in a totally unexpected direction, as you will see when you read this book. So, congratulations Los Angeles Rams, here we are!

Now that we know Jesus wasn't saying, "I'm sending out weaklings who can't protect themselves," which is how this scripture has been taught. Let's see what Jesus was actually saying. Rams don't eat meat, so wolves are not food (prey) for sheep. A sheep has no intention of harming a wolf. But wolves do eat meat, so rams are food (prey) for wolves. What Jesus was saying, then, is "I'm sending you out on a mission to save souls, but to those I'm sending you, you are food (prey). So, be as wise as a serpent (protect yourself if necessary)."

If you know anything about snakes, you'll know that most snakes won't attack you, but they will protect themselves and their territory.

Jesus also said, "And be as harmless as a dove (be led by the Holy Spirit)." That is, be discerning in your surroundings (know what's a threat and what's not).

Sheep are mentioned in the Bible more than 500 times, more than any other animal. The prominence of sheep in the Bible grows out of two realities. First, sheep were important to the nomads and agricultural life of the Hebrews and similar peoples. Secondly, sheep are used throughout the Bible to symbolically refer to God's people (us, The Body of Christ, The Children of God). My belief is, if I'm going to be called something, it's important for me to know something about it and why the comparison is being made.

Psalms 44:22 / Romans 8:36, As it is written:

"For your sake we face death all day long; we are considered as sheep to be slaughtered."

CHAPTER 1

Everything You Ever Wanted to Know About Sheep

Sheep were domesticated 10,000 years ago in Central Asia, and it was in 3,500 B.C. that people learned to spin wool. Sheep helped to make the spread of civilization possible, as we'll see below.

Sheep production was well-established during Biblical times. There are many references to sheep in the Bible, especially in the Old Testament. Sheep production is man's oldest organized industry.

Wool was the first commodity of sufficient value to warrant international trade. In the 1400s, Queen Isabella of Spain used money derived from the wool industry to finance Columbus and other conquistadors' voyages. In 1493, on his second voyage to the New World (America), Columbus took sheep with him as a "walking food supply." He left some sheep in Cuba and Santo Domingo.

In 1519, Cortez began his exploration of Mexico and what was to become the Western United States. He took with him sheep that were offspring of Columbus' sheep. These sheep are believed to be the ancestors of what are now called "Churros." The Navajo Churro is the oldest breed of sheep in the U.S. Despite efforts by the U.S. government to eradicate the breed, Navajo Churros are still raised by Navajo Indians.

The Gulf Coast (or Florida) Native is another breed of sheep believed to be directly descended from sheep brought to the New World by Spanish and French explorers.

During the 16th and 17th centuries, England tried to discourage the wool industry in the American colonies. Nonetheless, colonists quickly smuggled sheep into the New World and developed a wool industry. By 1664, there were 10,000 sheep in the colonies and the General Court of Massachusetts passed a law requiring youth to learn to spin and weave. By 1698, America was exporting wool goods.

England became outraged and outlawed wool trade, making it punishable by cutting off a person's right hand. The restrictions on sheep raising and wool manufacturing, along with the Stamp Act, led to the American Revolutionary War. Thus, spinning and weaving were considered patriotic acts. Even after the war, England enacted a law forbidding the export of any sheep but wethers (castrated rams).

George Washington raised sheep on his Mt. Vernon estate. Thomas Jefferson kept sheep at Monticello. Presidents Washington and Jefferson were both inaugurated in suits made of American wool. James Madison's inaugural jacket was woven from wool of sheep raised in his home in Virginia. President Woodrow Wilson grazed sheep on the White House lawn.

Sheep raising has played a role in several historical conflicts such as the "Highland Clearance," the American range wars, and the English "enclosing of the commons." The Highland Clearances consisted of the replacement of an almost feudal system of land tenure in Scotland with the rearing of sheep. Thousands of people were forced to leave their homes. In the U.S. range wars, violent conflicts erupted between cattle ranchers and sheep herders as they competed for land upon which to graze their livestock. Britain's close of the commons was similar to the Highland Clearance: Open fields were enclosed into individually owned fields for sheep farming, displacing many subsistence farmers.

Domesticated sheep are prey animals. When they are faced with danger, their instinct is to flee, not fight. Their strategy is to use avoidance and rapid flight to avoid being eaten. Some primitive sheep breeds are able to evade predators more effectively, as their natural instincts are stronger. Domesticated sheep have come to rely on man for protection from predators.

After fleeing, sheep will reform into groups and watch the predator. They use their natural herding instinct to band together for safety. A sheep that is by itself is vulnerable to attack.

Sheep tracks are never straight. Their winding trails allow sheep to observe what is behind them, first with one eye, then the other. Sheep can spot dogs or other perceived forms of danger from 1,200 to 1,500 yards away.

Sheep have excellent senses. Their wide angle of vision allows them to see predators on all sides. They can direct their ears in the direction of sounds. They are very sensitive to what different predators smell like. Sheep have an amazing tolerance for pain. They do not show pain, because if they do, they will be more vulnerable to predators who look for those who are weak or injured.

Sheep in the Bible
Why have I taken so much time discussing the history of sheep? As I mentioned earlier, sheep are mentioned in

the Bible more than 500 times, more than any other animal. The prominence of sheep in the Bible grows out of two realities. First, sheep were important to the nomads and agricultural life of the Hebrews and similar peoples. Secondly, sheep are used throughout the Bible to symbolically refer to God's people (us, The Body of Christ, The Children of God). Let's continue.

> Genesis 4:3-4, Now Abel kept flocks, and Cain worked the soil. In the course of time Cain brought some of the fruits of the soil as an offering to the Lord. But Abel also brought an offering, fat portions from some of the firstborn of his flock.

The very first shepherd was Abel. He was also humanity's first murder victim, slain by his brother Cain. Abraham and Moses were shepherds. King David was the best-known shepherd of Bible history. He wrote the beloved Psalm 23. Shepherds were the first people to see the newborn Jesus Christ.

> John 10:27, My sheep listen to my voice; I know them, and they follow me.

The Bible describes close relationships between shepherds and their flocks. The sheep recognize the voice of the shepherd. They follow him. The shepherd protects his flock and would give his life for them. It is known that animals can instantly recognize the voice of a familiar trusted person. Sheep have excellent memories for faces. They remember their handler. They also remember people who inflict abuse upon them.

Our next story of Biblical sheep needs its own chapter.

CHAPTER 2

The Story of Abraham

Genesis 22:1-18, Abraham looked up and there in a thicket he saw a ram caught by its horns. He went over and took the ram and sacrificed it as a burnt offering instead of his son.

It is well-known that Abraham was asked to sacrifice his son. He was willing to do so, but God gave him a sheep (ram) to sacrifice instead of his son. This is a widely misunderstood part of scripture that the enemy has used to question God's character and throw shade on God's name.

Let's take a closer look at this situation. In Genesis 12:1-4 the Bible says, "Now (in Haran) the Lord had said to Abram, 'Go away from your country and from your relatives and from your father's house, to the land which I will show you; and I will make you a great nation, and I will bless you (abundantly), and make your name great (exalted, distinguished); and you shall be a blessing (a source of great good to others); and I will bless (do good for, benefit) those who bless you, and I will curse (that is, subject to my wrath and judgment) the one who curses (despises, dishonors, has contempt for) you. And in you all the families (nations) of the earth will be blessed.'

"So, Abram departed (in faithful obedience) as the Lord had directed him; and Lot (his nephew) left with him. Abram was seventy-five years old when he left Haran. Abram took Sarai his wife and Lot his nephew, and all their possessions which they had acquired, and the people (servants) which they had acquired in Haran, and they set out to go to the land of Canaan."

Genesis 17:1 says, "When Abram was ninety-nine years old, the Lord appeared to him and said, 'I am God Almighty: walk (habitually) before Me (with integrity, knowing that you are always in My presence), and be blameless and complete (in obedience to Me). I will establish My covenant (everlasting promise) between Me and you, and I will multiply you exceedingly (through your descendants).'

"Then Abram fell on his face (in worship), and God spoke with him, saying, 'As for Me, behold, My covenant is with you, and (as a result) you shall be the father of many nations. No longer shall your name be Abram (exalted father), but your name shall be Abraham (father of a multitude); For I will make you the father of many nations. I will make you exceedingly fruitful, and I will make nations of you, and kings will come from you. I will establish My covenant between Me and you and your descendants after you throughout their generations for an everlasting covenant, to be God to you and to your descendants after you. I will give to you and to your descendants after you the land in which you are a stranger (moving from place to place), all the land of Canaan, as an everlasting possession (of property); and I will be their God.'"

Genesis 17:15-22 reads,

"Then God said to Abraham, 'As for Sarai your wife, you shall not call her name Sarai (my princess), but her name will be Sarah (Princess). I will bless her, and indeed I will also give you a son by her. Yes, I will bless her, and she shall be a mother of nations; kings of peoples will come from her.'

"Then Abraham fell on his face and laughed, and said in his heart, 'Shall a child be born to a man who is a hundred years old? And shall Sarah, who is ninety years old, bear a child?' And Abraham said to God, 'Oh, that Ishmael (my firstborn) might live before You!' But God said, 'No, Sarah your wife shall bear you a son indeed, and you shall name him Isaac (laughter); and I will establish My covenant with him for an everlasting covenant and with his descendants after him. As for Ishmael, I have heard and listened to you; behold, I will bless him, and will make him fruitful and will greatly multiply him (through his descendants). He will be the father of twelve princes (chieftains, sheiks), and I will make him a great nation. But My covenant (My promise, My solemn pledge), I will establish with Isaac, whom Sarah will bear to you at this time next year.' And God finished speaking with him and went up from Abraham."

Ishmael was Abraham's oldest son. We have to back track a little to make sure there is a clear understanding of these passages.

Genesis 15:1-7 says,

"After these things the Word of the Lord came to Abram in a vision, saying, 'Do not be afraid, Abram, I am your shield; Your reward (for obedience) shall be very great.' Abram said, 'Lord God, what reward will You give me, since I am (leaving this world) childless, and he who will be the owner and heir of my house is this (servant) Eliezer from Damascus?' And Abram continued, 'Since You have given no child to me, one (a servant) born in my house is my heir.'

"Then behold, the Word of the Lord came to him, saying, 'This man (Eliezer) will not be your heir but he who shall come from your own body shall be your heir; And the Lord brought Abram outside (his tent into the night) and said, 'Look now toward the heavens and count the stars, if you are able to count them.' Then God said to Abram, 'So (numerous) shall your descendants be.' Then Abram believed in (affirmed, trusted in, relied on, remained steadfast to) the Lord; and God counted (credited) it to Abram as righteousness (doing right in regard to God and man). And God said to Abram, 'I am the (same) Lord who brought you out of Ur of the Chaldeans, to give you this land as an inheritance.'"

Now let's head to chapter 16:1-15:

"Now Sarai, Abram's wife had not borne him any children, and she had an Egyptian maid whose name was Hagar. So, Sarai said to Abram, 'See here, the Lord has prevented me from bearing children. I am asking you to go in to (the bed of) my maid (so that she may bear you a child); perhaps I will obtain children by her.' And Abram listened to Sarai and did as she said. After Abram had lived in the land of Canaan ten years, Abram's wife Sarai took Hagar the Egyptian (maid) and gave her to her husband Abram to be his (secondary) wife. He went in to (the bed of) Hagar, and she conceived; and when she realized that she had conceived, she looked with contempt on her mistress (regarding Sarai as insignificant because of her infertility).

"Then Sarai said to Abram, 'May (the responsibility for) the wrong done to me (by the arrogant behavior of Hagar) be upon you. I gave my maid into your arms, and when she realized that she had conceived, I was despised and looked on with disrespect. May the Lord judge (who has done right) between you and me.' But Abram said to Sarai, 'look, your maid is entirely in your hands and subject to your authority; do as you please with her.' So, Sarai treated her harshly and humiliated her, and Hagar fled from her.

"But the Angel of the Lord found her by a spring of water in the wilderness, on the road to (Egypt by way of) Shur. And He said, 'Hagar, Sarai's maid, where did you come from and where are you going?' And she said, 'I am running away from my mistress Sarai.' The Angel of the Lord said to her, 'Go back to your mistress, and submit humbly to her authority.'

"Then the Angel of the Lord said to her, 'I will greatly multiply your descendants so that they will be too many to count.' The Angel of the Lord continued, 'Behold, you are with child, and you will bear a son; and you shall name him Ishmael (God hears), because the Lord has heard and paid attention to your persecution (suffering). He (Ishmael) will be a wild donkey of a man; His hand will be against every man (continually fighting) and every man's hand against him; And he will dwell in defiance of all his brothers.'

"Then she called the name of the Lord who spoke to her, 'You are God Who Sees,' for she said, 'Have I not even here (in the wilderness) remained alive after seeing Him (who sees me with understanding and compassion)?' Therefore, the well was called Beer-lahai-roi (Well of the Living One Who Sees Me); it is between Kadesh and Bered. So, Hagar gave birth to Abram's son; and Abram named his son, to whom Hagar gave birth, Ishmael (God hears). Abram was eighty-six years old when Hagar gave birth to Ishmael."

Okay, so let's catch back up. Genesis 21:1-7 says,

"The Lord graciously remembered and visited Sarah as He had said, and the Lord did for her as He had promised. So, Sarah conceived and gave birth to a son for Abraham in his old age, at the appointed time of which God had spoken to him. Abraham named his son Isaac (laughter), the son to whom Sarah gave birth. So, Abraham circumcised his son Isaac when he was eight days old, just as God had commanded him. Abraham was a hundred years old when his son Isaac was born. Sarah said, 'God has made me laugh; all who hear (about our good news) will laugh with me.' And she said, 'Who would have said to Abraham that Sarah would nurse children? For I have given birth to a son by him in his old age.' The child (Isaac) grew and was weaned, and Abraham held a great feast on the day that Isaac was weaned."

Now, by chapter 22, Abraham has had to send Ishmael and Hagar away and Isaac is a grown man. Genesis 22:1 says,

"Now after these things, God tested (the faith and commitment of) Abraham and said to him, 'Abraham!' And he answered, 'Here I am.' God said, 'Take now your son, your only son (of promise), whom you love, Isaac, and go to the region of Moriah, and offer him there as a burnt offering on one of the mountains of which I shall tell you.'"

The Son of the Promise
Abraham was 100 and Sarah was 90 when Sarah bore Abraham a son, Isaac the son of the promise. Sarah was barren and could not have children. God had closed her womb. At 90 her womb was considered dead. Abraham knew from this that God was able to bring life to dead things, and he believed that if God asked him to sacrifice His promised son, God could and would bring Isaac back to life.

Abraham trusted in God's goodness. God had, prior to this, told Abraham to send away his oldest son Ishmael. The son he had with Hagar, the maidservant of his wife Sarah, is Sarah's attempt to provide a solution to God's unbelievable promise of her bearing a son for Abraham. But this was not the son God promised, and Hagar was not the woman this promise was intended to come through.

Abraham loved Ishmael! Can you imagine how hard it must have been for Abraham to send his son away, and now God is telling him he must sacrifice his youngest son? Ishmael was gone, so Abraham had to believe God could, and would, give Isaac back, or I just can't see where he would have had it in him to say yes to God's request.

Why is God tempting Abraham like this? I hear you, this is not right! God is just toying with him. James 1:13 says, "when tempted no one should say God is tempting me. For God cannot be tempted by evil, nor does He tempt anyone." But God will test us from time to time, so that we can see what we are made of. God already knows, so He tests us so that we will also know.

God tests Abraham and tells him to sacrifice Isaac, his promised son.

Genesis 22:1-3 says,

> "Now after these things, God tested (the faith and commitment of) Abraham and said to him, 'Abraham!' And he answered, 'Here I am.' God said, 'Take now your son, your only son (of promise), whom you love, Isaac, and go to the region of Moriah, and offer him there as a burnt offering on one of the mountains of which I shall tell you.'
>
> "So, Abraham got up early in the morning, saddled his donkey, and took two of his young men with him and his son Isaac; and he split the wood for the burnt offering, and then he got up and went to the place of which God had told him."

Now, if we go back to verse 2 God tells Abraham "Take now your son." But in verse 3 it says, "So Abraham got up early in the morning." Then it says, "and he (Abraham) split the wood for the burnt offering." Do you know how long it would take for a 120 to 130+ year old man to cut enough wood to lay under a full-grown man?

Isaac was not a child at this time. There are some discrepancies about exactly how old he was, but there is no doubt he was not a child. Which brings us to something even more profound that I will get into later, which is the obedience of Isaac to his father.

Abraham stalled as long as he could, more than likely praying that God would give him some follow up instructions, like "April fools! I was just kidding!"

But obviously God wasn't kidding. So, the Bible says, "and then he (Abraham) got up and went to the place of which God had told him."

In order to get up he had to have been sitting down. After cutting wood Abraham sat down. It's talked about like God told Abraham to sacrifice his son Isaac, and Abraham just immediately jumped up and said yes Lord, I'll go. But as I read it, I see this waying heavy on Abraham's heart and I see Abraham taking a long time to provide a heartfelt yes. In fact, I don't know if he ever gave a heartfelt yes. I know he was obedient, but I'm not sure Abraham was feeling this. Abraham was God's guy, there is no doubt about that, but I believe Abraham was taking every step as slowly as possible to give God time to change His mind.

It took 3 days for them to get to the proper location:

"On the 3rd day (of travel) Abraham looked up and saw the place in the distance. Abraham said to his servants, 'Settle down and stay here with the donkey; the young man and I will go over there and worship (show the worth of, demonstrate how important someone or something is to you) (God), and we will come back to you.'

"Then Abraham took the wood for the burnt offering and laid it on (the shoulders of) Isaac his son, and he took the fire (firepot) in his own hand and the (sacrificial) knife; and the two of them walked on together. And Isaac said to Abraham, 'My father!' And he said, 'Here I am, my son.' Isaac said, 'Look, the fire and the wood, but where is the lamb for the burnt offering?' Abraham said, 'My son, God will provide for Himself a lamb for the burnt offering: So, the two walked on together.'"

CHAPTER 2

The Bible says in Amos 3:3, "Can two walk together, except they be agreed?" Isaac was not a child. So, I don't believe it was just a coincidence that it was put in the "Word of God" that Abraham and Isaac walked together after the conversation about the missing lamb. I believe Isaac was being just as obedient as his father Abraham.

The Bible also says in Amos 3:7, "Surely the Lord God does nothing without revealing His secret plan (of the judgment to come) to His servants the prophets."

It is my understanding that God was revealing to Abraham and to Isaac a foreshadowing of His plan of salvation. After this you don't hear much from Isaac in the Bible. This was Isaac's purpose; this was Isaac's call: To be obedient to his father, even unto death. Just as Jesus The Christ was obedient to His Father (God) even unto death. "Not My Will, but Your Will be done."

When God was going to destroy Sodom and Gomorrah, He told Abraham about it and Abraham pleaded with God. Abraham ended his plea with this (Genesis 18:32): "Then Abraham said, 'Oh may the Lord not be angry (with me), and I will speak only this once. Suppose ten (righteous people) are found there?' And God said, 'I will not destroy it for the sake of the ten.'"

In the time of Noah, the Bible states in Genesis 6:5, "The Lord saw that the wickedness (depravity) of man was great on the earth, and that every imagination or intent of the thoughts of his heart were only evil continually." But God found one man, Noah, to be righteous. So, God destroyed the rest of the world and started over with Noah and Noah's family.

There is a powerful reason that Abraham was Chosen to be the Father of The Promise. There is also an amazing reason why Isaac was Chosen to be the Son of The

Promise. Abraham and Isaac were Called to be a foreshadowing of God The Father and God The Son, and they both answered the Call with Obedience, even unto death.

The Sacrifice
Every other god worshipped in this part of the world at the time of Abraham and Isaac demanded the sacrifice of a human child. Why?

We read in the first 5 chapters of Leviticus about burnt offerings, grain offerings, peace offerings, sin offerings, and the guilt offering. The offerings you make to God should be the best you have. In Malachi, God says, "you treat me with contempt." They ask how? God says, "you give me your leftovers."

So, trying to pull a one up on God, these other gods, who were really no gods at all, demanded the best you have. And what is the very best you have? Your firstborn son! God uses this opportunity to show that He is not like these other gods. God separates Himself. God is saying to Abraham and Isaac, "I am not like this I would never demand for you to do something like this. I would offer myself first, as He did on the cross."

Genesis 22:9 reads,

> "When they came to the place of which God had told him, Abraham built an altar there and arranged the wood, and bound Isaac his son and placed him on the altar, on top of the wood. Abraham reached out his hand and took the knife to kill his son.
>
> "But the Angel of the Lord called to him from heaven and said, 'Abraham, Abraham!' He answered, 'Here I am.' The Lord said, 'Do not reach out (with the

knife in) your hand against the boy and do nothing to (harm) him; for now, I know that you fear God (with reverence and profound respect), since you have not withheld from Me your son, your only son (of promise).'

"Then Abraham looked up and glanced around, and behold, behind him was a ram caught in a thicket by his horns. And Abraham named that place The Lord Will Provide. And it is said to this day, 'On the mountain of the Lord it will be seen and provided.'

"The Angel of the Lord called to Abraham from heaven a second time and said, 'By Myself (on the basis of Who I Am) I have sworn (an oath), declares the Lord, that since you have done this thing and have not withheld (from Me) your son, your only son (of promise), indeed I will greatly bless you, and I will greatly multiply your descendants like the stars of the heavens and like the sand on the seashore; and your seed shall possess the gate of their enemies (as conquerors). Through your seed all the nations of the earth shall be blessed, because you have heard and obeyed My voice.' So, Abraham returned to his servants, and they got up and went with him to Beersheba; and Abraham settled in Beersheba."

Though he was also obedient, I don't know if Isaac had as deep an understanding about this whole situation. Abraham said to his servants, "Settle down and stay here with the donkey; the young man and I will go over there and worship (show the worth of, demonstrate how important someone or something is to you) (God), and we will come back to you."

But after the Angel of the Lord spoke to Abraham a second time the Bible says, "So Abraham returned to his servants, and they got up and went with him to Beersheba; and Abraham settled in Beersheba."

It doesn't mention Isaac coming back with Abraham. Remember, Isaac was a grown man, not a child. I don't know if Abraham and Isaac's relationship was the same after this. I'm not sure whether Isaac or Abraham knew what they were being obedient to. We have the Bible so we can look at things in hindsight, but they were living this in the moment, making it a whole lot harder for them to understand.

I feel that it is necessary to show the humanity of Abraham and Isaac, because we are called to walk in obedience as well. And although a lot of the times it's not easy or understandable, it's always necessary. That's why it's called faith. Although these men didn't understand the significance of what they were doing at the time, today we can look at their life and understand what God is doing in *our* lives when He tests us.

In Faith We Go
Hebrews 11:8 says, "By faith Abraham when called to go to a place he would later receive as his inheritance obeyed and went. Even though he didn't know where he was going. By faith he made his home in the promised land like a stranger in a strange land. He lived in tents as did Isaac and Jacob who were heirs with him of the same promise. For he was looking forward to the city with foundations, who's architect and builder is God."

Verse 17 says, "By faith Abraham, when he was tested (that is, as the testing of his faith was still in progress), offered up Isaac, and he who had received the promises (of God) was ready to sacrifice his only son (of promise); to who it was said, 'Through Isaac your descendants shall be called.' For he considered (it reasonable to believe) that God was able to raise Isaac even from among the dead.'"

1 Corinthians 15:1-5 says,

> "Now brothers and sisters, let me remind you (once again) of the good news (of salvation) which I preached to you, which you welcomed and accepted and on which you stand (by faith). By this faith you are saved (reborn from above-spiritually transformed, renewed, and set apart for His purpose), if you hold firmly to the word which I preached to you, unless you believed in vain (just superficially and without complete commitment). For I passed on to you as of first importance what I also received, that Christ died for our sins according to (that which) the Scriptures (foretold), and that He appeared to Cephas (Peter), then to the Twelve."

1 Corinthians 15:12-28 says,

> "Now if Christ is preached as raised from the dead, how is it that some among you say that there is no resurrection of the dead? But if there is no resurrection of the dead, then not even Christ has been raised; and if Christ has not been raised, then our preaching is vain (useless, amounting to nothing), and your faith is also vain (imaginary, unfounded, devoid of value and benefit, not based on truth). We are even discovered to be false witnesses (misrepresenting) God because we testified concerning Him that He raised Christ, whom He did not raise, if in fact the dead are not raised. For if the dead are not raised, then Christ has not been raised, either; and if Christ has not been raised your faith is worthless and powerless (mere delusion); you

are still in your sins (and under the control and penalty of sin). Then those also who have fallen asleep in Christ are lost. If we who are (abiding) in Christ have hoped only in this life (and this is all there is), then we are of all people most miserable and to be pitied.

"But now (as things really are) Christ has in fact been raised from the dead, (and He became) the first fruits (that is, the first to be resurrected with an incorruptible, immortal body, foreshadowing the resurrection) of those who have fallen asleep (in death). For since (it was) by a man that death came (into the world), it is also by a Man that the resurrection of the dead has come. For just as in Adam all die, so also in Christ all will be made alive. But each in his own order: Christ the first fruits, then those who are Christ's (own will be resurrected with incorruptible, immortal bodies) at His coming. After that comes the end (completion), when He hands over the Kingdom to God the Father, after He has made inoperative and abolished every ruler and every authority and power.

"For Christ must reign (as King) until He has put all His enemies under His feet. The last enemy to be abolished and put to an end is death. For He (the Father) Has put all things in subjection under His (Christ's) feet. But when He says, 'All things have been put in subjection (under Christ),' it is clear that He (the Father) who put all things in subjection to Him (Christ), then the Son Himself will also be subject to the One (the Father) who put all things in subjection to Him (Christ) is excepted (since the Father is not in subjection to His own Son). However, when all things are subjected to Him (Christ), then the Son Himself will also be subjected to the One (the Father) who put all things under Him, so that God maybe all in all (manifesting His glory without any opposition, the supreme indwelling and controlling factor of life).""

Galatians 3:6-8 says,

"Just as Abraham believed God, and it was credited to him as righteousness, (as conformity to God's will and purpose, so it is with you also). So, understand that it is the people who live by faith (with confidence in the power and goodness of God) who are (the true) sons of Abraham. The Scripture, foreseeing that God would justify the Gentiles by faith, proclaimed the good news (of the Savior) to Abraham in advance (with this promise), saying, 'In you shall all the nations be blessed.' So, then those who are people of faith (whether Jew or Gentile) are blessed and favored by God (and declared free of the guilt of sin and its penalty and placed in right standing with Him) along with Abraham, the believer."

The Good News

We read in Galatians 3:8, "The Scripture, foreseeing that God would justify the Gentiles by faith, proclaimed the good news (of the Savior) to Abraham in advance (with this promise), saying, 'In you shall al the nations be blessed.'"

Where and when did God proclaim the good news (of the Savior) to Abraham?

God appears to Abraham 7 times in his life: Genesis 12:1, Genesis 12:6, Genesis 13:14, Genesis 15:1 Genesis 17:1, Genesis 18:1, Genesis 22.

Genesis 12:1

God first appears to Abraham in Genesis 12:1: "Now (in Haran) the Lord had said to Abram, 'Go away from your country, and from your relatives and from your father's house, to the land which I will show you; And I will make you a great nation, and I will bless you (abundantly), and make your name great (exalted, distinguished); And you shall be a blessing (a source of great good to others); And I will bless (do good for, benefit) those who bless you, and I will curse (that is, subject to My wrath and judgment) the one who curses (despises, dishonors, has contempt for) you. And in you all the families (nations) of the earth will be blessed.'"

Here God discusses how He will bless Abraham if he is willing to leave his country and his father's house and go where He will show him.

Genesis 12:6-7.

Genesis 12:6-7 says, "Abram passed through the land as far as the site of Shechem, to the (great) terebinth (oak) tree of Moreh. Now the Canaanites were in the land at that time. Then the Lord appeared to Abram and said, 'I will give this land to your descendants.' So, Abram built an altar there to (honor) the Lord who had appeared to him."

Nothing about Salvation in this passage. This instance of appearing was about property and inheritance.

Genesis 13:14-18

Genesis 13:14-18 says,

> "The Lord said to Abram, after Lot had left him, 'Now lift up your eyes and look from the place where you are standing, northward and southward and eastward and westward, for all the land which you

see I will give to you and to your descendants forever. I will make your descendants (as numerous) as the dust of the earth, so that if a man could count the (grains of) dust of the earth, then your descendants could also be counted. Arise, walk (make a thorough reconnaissance) around in the land, through its length and its width, for I will give it to you.' Then Abram broke camp and moved his tent and came and settled by the (grove of the great) terebinths (oak trees) of Mamre (the Amorite), which are in Hebron, and there he built an altar to (honor) the Lord."

More about property, legacy, and inheritance. Again, nothing about Salvation.

Genesis 15:1
Genesis 15:1 says,

"After these things the word of the Lord came to Abram in a vision, saying, 'Do not be afraid, Abram, I am your shield; Your reward [for obedience] shall be very great.' Abram said, 'Lord God, what reward will You give me, since I am [leaving this world] childless, and he who will be the owner and heir of my house is this [servant] Eliezer from Damascus?' And Abram continued, 'Since You have given no child to me, one (a servant) born in my house is my heir.'

"Then behold, the word of the Lord came to him, saying, 'This man [Eliezer] will not be your heir but he who shall come from your own body shall be your heir.' And the Lord brought Abram outside [his tent into the night] and said, 'Look now toward the heavens and count the stars if you are able to count them.' Then He said to him, 'So [numerous] shall your descendants be.'

"Then Abram believed in (affirmed, trusted in, relied on, remained steadfast to) the Lord; and He counted (credited) it to him as righteousness (doing right in regard to God and man). And He said to him, 'I am the [same] Lord who brought you out of Ur of the Chaldeans, to give you this land as an inheritance.' But Abram said, 'Lord God, by what [proof] will I know that I will inherit it?' So, God said to him, 'Bring Me a three-year-old heifer, a three-year-old female goat, a three-year-old ram, a turtledove, and a young pigeon.' So, Abram brought all these to Him and cut them down the middle and laid each half opposite the other; but he did not cut the birds. The birds of prey swooped down on the carcasses, but Abram drove them away.

"When the sun was setting, a deep sleep overcame Abram; and a horror (terror, shuddering fear, nightmare) of great darkness overcame him. God said to Abram, 'Know for sure that your descendants will be strangers [living temporarily] in a land (Egypt) that is not theirs, where they will be enslaved and oppressed for four hundred years. But on that nation whom your descendants will serve I will bring judgment, and afterward they will come out [of that land] with great possessions. As for you, you shall [die and] go to your fathers in peace; you shall be buried at a good old age. Then in the fourth generation your descendants shall return here [to Canaan, the land of promise], for the wickedness and guilt of the Amorites is not yet complete (finished).'

"When the sun had gone down and a [deep] darkness had come, there appeared a smoking brazier and a flaming torch which passed between the [divided] pieces [of the animals]. On the same day the Lord made a covenant (promise, pledge) with Abram, saying, 'To your descendants I have given this land, From the river of Egypt to the great river Euphrates [the land of] the Kenites and the Kenizzites and the Kadmonites and the Hittites and the Perizzites and the Rephaim, the Amorites and the Canaanites and the Girgashites and the Jebusites.'"

Once again, nothing here about Salvation. Only more about property, legacy, and inheritance.

Genesis 17:1-22
Genesis 17:1-22 says,

> "When Abram was ninety-nine years old, the Lord appeared to him and said, 'I am God Almighty; Walk [habitually] before Me [with integrity, knowing that you are always in My presence], and be blameless and complete [in obedience to Me]. I will establish My covenant (everlasting promise) between Me and you, And I will multiply you exceedingly [through your descendants].'

> "Then Abram fell on his face [in worship], and God spoke with him, saying, 'As for Me, behold, My covenant is with you, and [as a result] you shall be the father of many nations. No longer shall your name be Abram (exalted father), But your name shall be Abraham (father of a multitude); For I will make you the father of many nations. I will make you exceedingly fruitful, and I will make nations of you, and kings will come from you. I will establish My covenant between Me and you and your descendants after you throughout their generations for an everlasting covenant, to be God to you and to your descendants after you. I will give to you and to your descendants after you the land in which you are a stranger [moving

from place to place], all the land of Canaan, as an everlasting possession [of property]; and I will be their God.'

"Further, God said to Abraham, 'As for you [your part of the agreement], you shall keep and faithfully obey [the terms of] My covenant, you and your descendants after you throughout their generations. This is [the sign of] My covenant, which you shall keep and faithfully obey, between Me and you and your descendants after you: Every male among you shall be circumcised. And you shall be circumcised in the flesh of your foreskins, and it shall be the sign (symbol, memorial) of the covenant between Me and you. Every male among you who is eight days old shall be circumcised throughout your generations, [including] a servant whether born in the house or one who is purchased with [your] money from any foreigner, who is not of your descendants.

"'A servant who is born in your house or one who is purchased with your money must be circumcised; and [the sign of] My covenant shall be in your flesh for an everlasting covenant. And the male who is not circumcised in the flesh of his foreskin, that person shall be cut off from his people; he has broken My covenant.'

"Then God said to Abraham, 'As for Sarai your wife, you shall not call her name Sarai (my princess), but her name will be Sarah (Princess). I will bless her, and indeed I will also give you a son by her. Yes, I will bless her, and she shall be a mother of nations; kings of peoples will come from her.' Then Abraham fell on his face and laughed, and said in his heart, 'Shall a child be born to a man who is a hundred years old? And shall Sarah, who is ninety years old, bear a child?'

"And Abraham said to God, 'Oh, that Ishmael [my firstborn] might live before You!' But God said, 'No, Sarah your wife shall bear you a son indeed, and you shall name him Isaac (laughter); and I will establish My covenant with him for an everlasting covenant and with his descendants after him. As for Ishmael, I have heard and listened to you; behold, I will bless him, and will make him fruitful and will greatly multiply him [through his descendants]. He will be the father of twelve princes (chieftains, sheiks), and I will make him a great nation. But My covenant [My promise, My solemn pledge], I will establish with Isaac, whom Sarah will bear to you at this time next year.' And God finished speaking with him and went up from Abraham.

"Then Abraham took Ishmael his son, and all the servants who were born in his house and all who were purchased with his money, every male among the men of Abraham's household, and circumcised the flesh of their foreskin the very same day, as God had said to him. So, Abraham was ninety-nine years old when he was circumcised. And Ishmael his son was thirteen years old when he was circumcised. On the very same day Abraham was circumcised, as well as Ishmael his son. All the men [servants] of his household, both those born in the house and those purchased with money from a foreigner, were circumcised along with him [as the sign of God's covenant with Abraham]."

Nothing here about Salvation. Here we have Covenant and more about property, legacy, and inheritance.

Genesis 18:1

Genesis 18:1 says,

"Now the Lord appeared to Abraham by the terebinth trees of Mamre [in Hebron], while he was sitting at the tent door in the heat of the day. When he raised his eyes and looked up, behold, three men were standing [a little distance] from him. When he saw them, he ran from the tent door to meet them and bowed down [with his face] to the ground, and Abraham said, 'My lord, if now I have found favor in your sight, please do not pass by your servant [without stopping to visit]. Please let a little water be brought [by one of my servants] and [you may] wash your feet and recline and rest comfortably under the tree. And I will bring a piece of bread to refresh and sustain you; after that you may go on, since you have come to your servant.' And they replied, 'Do as you have said.' So, Abraham hurried into the tent to Sarah, and said, 'Quickly, get ready three measures of fine meal, knead it and bake cakes.' Abraham also ran to the herd and brought a calf, tender and choice, and he gave it to the servant [to butcher], and he hurried to prepare it. Then he took curds and milk and the calf which he had prepared and set it before the men; and he stood beside them under the tree while they ate.

"Then they said to him, 'Where is Sarah your wife?' And he said, 'There, in the tent.' He said, 'I will surely return to you at this time next year; and behold, Sarah your wife will have a son.' And Sarah was listening at the tent door, which was behind him. Now Abraham and Sarah were old, well advanced in years; she was past [the age of] childbearing. So, Sarah laughed to herself [when she heard the Lord's words], saying, 'After I have become old, shall I have pleasure and delight, my lord (husband) being also old?' And the Lord asked Abraham, 'Why did Sarah laugh [to herself], saying, "Shall I really give birth [to a child] when I am so old?" Is anything too difficult or too wonderful for the Lord? At the appointed time, when the season [for her delivery] comes, I will return to you and Sarah will have a son.' Then Sarah denied it, saying, 'I did not laugh;' because she was afraid. And He (the Lord) said, 'No, but you did laugh.'

"Then the men got up from there and looked toward Sodom; and Abraham walked with them to send them on the way. The Lord said, 'Shall I keep secret from Abraham [My friend and servant] what I am going to do, since Abraham is destined to become a great and mighty nation, and all the nations of the earth will be blessed through him? For I have known (chosen, acknowledged) him [as My own], so that he may teach and command his children and [the sons of] his household after him to keep the way of the Lord by doing what is righteous and just, so that the Lord may bring upon Abraham what He has promised him.' And the Lord said, 'The outcry [of the sin] of Sodom and Gomorrah is indeed great, and their sin is exceedingly grave. I will go down now and see whether they have acted [as vilely and wickedly] as the outcry which has come to Me [indicates]; and if not, I will know.'

"Now the [two] men (angelic beings) turned away from there and went toward Sodom, but Abraham remained standing before the Lord. Abraham approached [the Lord] and said, 'Will You really sweep away the righteous (those who do right) with the wicked (those who do evil)? Suppose there are fifty righteous [people] within the city; will You really sweep it away and not spare it for the sake of the fifty righteous who are in it? Far be it from You to do such a thing, to strike the righteous with the wicked, so that the righteous and the wicked are treated alike. Far be it from You! Shall not the Judge of all the earth do right [by executing just and righteous judgment]?'

"So, the Lord said, 'If I find within the city of Sodom fifty righteous [people], then I will spare the entire place for their sake.' Abraham answered, 'Now behold, I who am but dust [in origin] and ashes have decided to speak to the Lord. If five of the fifty righteous are lacking, will You destroy the entire city for lack of five?' And He said, 'If I find [at least] forty-five [righteous people] there, I will not destroy it.'

"Abraham spoke to Him yet again and said, 'Suppose [only] forty are found there.' And He said, 'I will not do it for the sake of the forty [who are righteous].' Then Abraham said [to Him], 'Oh, may the Lord not be angry, and I will speak; suppose thirty [righteous people] are found there?' And He said, 'I will not do it if I find thirty there.' And he said, 'Now behold, I have decided to speak to the Lord [again]. Suppose [only] twenty [righteous people] are found there?' And the Lord said, 'I will not destroy it for the sake of the twenty.' Then Abraham said, 'Oh may the Lord not be angry [with me], and I will speak only this once; suppose ten [righteous people] are found there?' And He said, 'I will not destroy it for the sake of the ten.' As soon as He had finished speaking with Abraham the Lord departed, and Abraham returned to his own place."

You may wonder, as I did, why Abraham didn't go to the obvious next request: "If there are five righteous people in the city, will you still destroy it?" See, Lot (Abraham's nephew), Lot's wife, Lot's two daughters, and their husbands were in the city as well (a total of six family members).

So, if Abraham went down to five righteous people, and God said He wouldn't destroy it for the sake of five, and then the city was destroyed, Abraham would know that his nephew and family were a part of the wickedness in Sodom and Gomorrah. I guess he decided not to test the water.

This appearance of the Lord starts off providing a date to God's promise given to Abraham and Sarah about having a child in their old age: The Promised Child. I don't see the events shown here as coincidental. The promise of a miracle son is to come from a barren woman (Sarah). Abraham then is told that God is going to destroy Sodom and Gomorrah because of the sins of the people. So what does Abraham, the "father of many nations," do? Intercedes on their behalf, pleading their case to God. How interesting this is seeing as how we only have one appearance left!

Genesis 22

Genesis 22 says,

> "Now after these things, God tested [the faith and commitment of] Abraham and said to him, 'Abraham!' And he answered, "Here I am.' God said, 'Take now your son, your only son [of promise], whom you love, Isaac, and go to the region of Moriah, and offer him there as a burnt offering on one of the mountains of which I shall tell you.' So, Abraham got up early in the morning, saddled his donkey, and took two of his young men with him and his son Isaac; and he split the wood for the burnt offering, and then he got up and went to the place of which God had told him.

"On the third day [of travel] Abraham looked up and saw the place in the distance. Abraham said to his servants, 'Settle down and stay here with the donkey; the young man and I will go over there and worship [God], and we will come back to you.' Then Abraham took the wood for the burnt offering and laid it on [the shoulders of] Isaac his son, and he took the fire (firepot) in his own hand and the [sacrificial] knife; and the two of them walked on together. And Isaac said to Abraham, 'My father!' And he said, 'Here I am, my son.' Isaac said, 'Look, the fire and the wood, but where is the lamb for the burnt offering?' Abraham said, 'My son, God will provide for Himself a lamb for the burnt offering.'

"So, the two walked on together. When they came to the place of which God had told him, Abraham built an altar there and arranged the wood, and bound Isaac his son and placed him on the altar, on top of the wood. Abraham reached out his hand and took the knife to kill his son. But the Angel of the Lord called to him from heaven and said, 'Abraham, Abraham!' He answered, 'Here I am.' The Lord said, 'Do not reach out [with the knife in] your hand against the boy and do nothing to [harm] him; for now, I know that you fear God [with reverence and profound respect], since you have not withheld from Me your son, your only son [of promise].'

"Then Abraham looked up and glanced around, and behold, behind him was a ram caught in a thicket by his horns. And Abraham went and took the ram and offered it up for a burnt offering (ascending sacrifice) instead of his son. So, Abraham named that place The Lord Will Provide. And it is said to this day, 'On the mountain of the Lord it will be seen and provided.'

"The Angel of the Lord called to Abraham from heaven a second time and said, 'By Myself (on the basis of Who I Am) I have sworn [an oath], declares the Lord, that since you have done this thing and have not withheld [from Me] your son, your only son [of promise], indeed I will greatly bless you, and I will greatly multiply your descendants like the stars of the heavens and like the sand on the seashore; and your seed shall possess the gate of their enemies [as conquerors]. Through your seed all the nations of the earth shall be blessed, because you have heard and obeyed My voice.' So, Abraham returned to his servants, and they got up and went with him to Beersheba; and Abraham settled in Beersheba."

Abraham is called to sacrifice his son, his firstborn son, his promised son, the son whom he loves. And why was Abraham able to do this? Because he has no feelings for his son? Of course not! He could do it because he believed that, just as God brought life to his body as good as dead, as it relates to childbearing and also life to Sarah's barren womb, that if God demanded Isaac's life, that same God could raise him back to life. But God never intended for Isaac to be sacrificed. Just as Abraham had spoken, God had a plan for Salvation. As Genesis 22:7-8 says, "And Isaac said to Abraham, 'My father!' And he said, 'Here I am, my son.' Isaac said, 'Look, the fire and the wood, but where is the lamb for the burnt offering?' Abraham said, 'My son, God will provide for Himself a lamb for the burnt offering.' So, the two walked on together."

Just as the Bible says, God does nothing without revealing it to His prophets. God chose Abraham to be the father of many nations, the father of promise. God said that through Abraham's seed all nations on earth would be blessed. So, God revealed to him exactly how Salvation would take place. Amos 3:7 says, "Surely the Lord God does nothing without revealing His secret plan [of the judgment to come] to His servants the prophets."

Genesis 22:15-18 says,

> "The Angel of the Lord called to Abraham from heaven a second time and said, 'By Myself (on the basis of Who I Am) I have sworn [an oath], declares the Lord, that since you have done this thing and have not withheld [from Me] your son, your only son [of promise], indeed I will greatly bless you, and I will greatly multiply your descendants like the stars of the heavens and like the sand on the seashore; and your seed shall possess the gate of their enemies [as conquerors]. Through your seed all the nations of the earth shall be blessed, because you have heard and obeyed My voice.'"

Hebrews 1:1-14 says,

> "God, having spoken to the fathers long ago in [the voices and writings of] the prophets in many separate revelations [each of which set forth a portion of the truth], and in many ways, has in these last days spoken [with finality] to us in [the person of One who is by His character and nature] His Son [namely Jesus], whom He appointed heir and lawful owner of all things, through whom also He created the universe [that is, the universe as a space-time-matter continuum]. The Son is the radiance and only expression of the glory of [our awesome] God [reflecting God's Shekinah glory, the Light-being, the brilliant light of the divine], and the exact representation and perfect

imprint of His [Father's] essence and upholding and maintaining and propelling all things [the entire physical and spiritual universe] by His powerful word [carrying the universe along to its predetermined goal].

"When He [Himself and no other] had [by offering Himself on the cross as a sacrifice for sin] accomplished purification from sins and established our freedom from guilt, He sat down [revealing His completed work] at the right hand of the Majesty on high [revealing His Divine authority], having become as much superior to angels, since He has inherited a more excellent and glorious name than they [that is, Son, the name above all names]. For to which of the angels did the Father ever say, 'You are My Son, today I have begotten (fathered) You [established You as a Son, with kingly dignity]'? And again [did He ever say to the angels], 'I shall be a Father to Him and He shall be a Son to Me?' And when He again brings the firstborn [highest-ranking Son] into the world, He says, 'And all the angels of God are to worship Him.'

"And concerning the angels He says, 'Who makes His angels winds, And His ministering servants flames of fire [to do His bidding].' But about the Son [the Father says to Him], 'Your throne, O God, is forever and ever, And the scepter of [absolute] righteousness is the scepter of His kingdom. You have loved righteousness [integrity, virtue, uprightness in purpose] and have hated lawlessness [injustice, sin]. Therefore God, Your God, has anointed You with the oil of gladness above Your companions.' And, 'You, Lord, laid the foundation of the earth in the beginning, And the heavens are the works of Your hands; They will perish, but You remain [forever and ever]; And they will all wear out like a garment, And like a robe You will roll them up; Like a garment they will be changed. But

You are the same [forever], And Your years will never end.' But to which of the angels has the Father ever said, 'Sit at My right hand [together with Me in royal dignity], until I make your enemies a footstool for Your feet [in triumphant conquest]'? Are not all the angels' ministering spirits sent out [by God] to serve (accompany, protect) those who will inherit salvation? [Of course they are!]."

God through the sacrifice of our Lord and Savior Jesus Christ has granted us a name to be revered, "Sons." Son is not gender specific; Son is a position. We are all, who accept Jesus Christ as our Lord and personal Savior, Sons of God. That includes male and female, and every color of person under the sun.

We as a whole have done and are still doing some terrible things in and to this world. But God has given us THE REMEDY, THE SOLUTION. What is it you might ask? THE KINGDOM OF GOD!

The Kingdom of God is the only solution to the problem to what this world is and will ever face. God has designed it that way, and as long as we continue to fight His plan, we will continue to see what looks to us like progress slowly turn toward utter destruction. God is not playing with us and, as quiet as this plan is kept, God is, and always has been, in complete control.

"Seek first the kingdom of God and His righteousness and all these things will be added." God is not saying this just to be saying something. He is letting us know how this world should be run. And the only way things will work out right is if we learn how to operate in this manner. "GOD WHAT DO YOU WANT US TO DO"?

Note that I didn't say the *problems* we are facing, I said *the* problem. Just as in Genesis 12:3a, God didn't say He would curse the ones or those who curse you. He said, "And I will bless (do good for, benefit) those who bless you." Why? Because they are listening to and doing what God wants them to do, whether they are aware of it or not. He said, "And I will curse (that is, subject to My wrath and judgment) the one who curses (despises, dishonors, has contempt for) you." Why does God say He will curse the one and not the others? Because we know not what we do!

There are only two influences. You are either on one side or the other, there is no neutral ground. Everyone, without exception, must choose a side! And since I know how the story ends, I choose the winning side! And I have been commissioned to make you aware of the deception and assist you in the choosing process.

CHAPTER 3

The Sheep and the Goats

He shall set the sheep on His right hand, but the goats on the left (Matthew 25:33).

Sheep and goats are used as a metaphor in the Bible in regard to Judgement Day. Sheep are the followers of Christ, while goats choose not to follow Christ. This parable is based on the differences in behavior between sheep and goats. The sheep are those who follow the leading and guidance of Jesus Christ. They follow the direction of the Holy Spirit, obeying the commands of the Father.

Three Parables of Matthew

The 10 virgins

Notice the parables given in Matthew 25. First, there are the 10 virgins, 5 foolish and 5 wise. What made the 5 foolish? They didn't have enough oil to keep their light shining (no true relationship with God, just enough for Sunday). What made the other 5 wise? They had more than enough stored up, enough to keep their light shining (an intimate relationship with God, every day is Sunday). They even had extra, but they were wise enough to know it wasn't to be shared with the 5 foolish virgins who were given the same opportunity and allotted time they were given.

The talents

The next parable discusses the talents given to servants by their master, who goes away on a journey. When the master comes back, he calls for his servants to see how profitable they have been with the talents he had given to them. To the first servant he gave 5 talents, and the servant doubled it and ended up with 10 talents, and the master was pleased. The second servant was given 2 talents, which he also doubled, and this also pleased the master. But the final servant who was given one talent had buried it. So then he went and dug it up and gave it to the master. The master was not pleased.

The scripture says that the master gave the servants the number of talents according to their abilities. So, he gave this servant only one talent. Everybody has to have some talent. It would be unfair if they did not. It would also be unfair to give someone more than they can handle. That's why he gave them talents according to their ability, how much the master knew they could handle.

The reasoning the servant gave for not utilizing the master's talent and adding to its value was, "I knew you to be a harsh and demanding man, reaping (the harvest) where you did not sow and gathering where you did not scatter seed. So, I was afraid (to lose the talent), and I went and hid your talent in the ground. See, you have what is your own."

The master calls the servant a wicked, lazy servant. Why? Because we're talking about Jesus here, not some earthy master that is just out for selfish greed and gain.

We are given our talents and abilities to be fruitful and multiply and to share in Gods Glory. No matter what you have or what you will accomplish, God has given you the talents and ability to do it. This is so even if you've used the talent (ability) that He's given you for immoral, unethical, or destructive purposes. You still can find a way to use that God-given talent (ability) to advance God's Kingdom.

Jesus knows our abilities and He also knows our heart. What the servant was saying is, "I'm not going to do all the work and you get the harvest (credit, accolades, reward, profit). I don't care what talent you gave me; I'll sit on it before I let you reap the rewards of it. I did this!"

But how? How did you do it? You didn't make your abilities yourself. Everything you have, or will ever accomplish, God gave you, even the tenacity and grit it took for you to climb out of some hole that you might be in. I know this doesn't seem fair, but God knew you would be in that hole, and that's why He gave you the abilities and talents you needed to get out.

There is no such thing as a self-made person. Everything you are or will ever be God has given you the ability to become, whether you used it to make something good or bad, positive, or negative. Any doors that were opened, it doesn't matter how hard you kicked to get them open. God gave you the strength it took to kick, and He made sure it was a door that your kick could open. I don't care how smart you are, how cunning and clever, or how good your gift of gab is. God allowed your business deals to go through, those plans to work, and for you to get the girl/guy.

Notice that the master didn't take the talents back, He just asked them about them. He also gave the talent that was not used to the servant with the most ability and talents. God will give you more, but you first have to be willing to use what He's already given you. Why would God give you more if you haven't utilized what you've already been given?

It's time to stop complaining about what we don't have and start working with what we do.

The coming of the Son of Man
The third parable speaks of the coming of the Son of Man, Jesus Christ in His glory and majesty and all the angels with Him. As He's seated on the throne of His glory, all the nations are gathered before Him (for judgement), and He separates them from one another, as a shepherd separates his sheep from the goats.

As Jesus begins to pronounce judgement, He does a surprising thing. He separates them not by the ten commandments or the strictness of the law, but by what they did or didn't do for those in need. Micah told the people that God's demands are clear and simple. Micah 6:6-8 says, "With what shall I come before the Lord (to honor Him) and bow myself before God on high? Shall I come before Him with burnt offerings, with yearling calves? Will the Lord be delighted with thousands of rams, or with ten thousand rivers of oil? Shall I present my firstborn for my acts of rebellion, the fruit of my body for the sin of my soul? He has told you, O man, what is good; And what does the Lord require of you except to be just, and to love (and to diligently practice) kindness (compassion), and to walk humbly with your God (setting aside any overblown sense of importance or self-righteousness)?"

Summarizing this, we must gain and stay in an intimate relationship with God (parable of the 10 virgins), so that we will have the wherewithal to use the ability(s) God has given us (parable of the talents), to help those in need and make this world a better place (parable of the sheep and the goats).

More on the Subject of Sheep
Stick with me, I'm going somewhere with all of this. Let's get back to the sheep. There was no information I could find on sheep before they were domesticated. All the information I found was on sheep with humans, that is, with a shepherd. I found nothing about how sheep survived before being under human guidance and authority. So, with that, let's take a look at the breeding process.

The "sheep year" begins in the middle of October when the rams are put in with the ewes for breeding. Only one ram is put in with a group of ewes so that the sire of all the lambs will be known. The rams are then switched into other pens after the first and second heat cycles in case some ewes do not become pregnant with the first ram.

With fall breeding, most ewes will get pregnant within the first 17 days of the breeding season. This is the average length of one estrus (heat) cycle. Fertility is high when breeding occurs during the most natural time (fall).

The flock will stay on pasture until the grass is depleted, usually around Christmas time, or earlier if it was a drought year. Lambing usually starts in the middle of March. Yearling ewes are bred to lamb three weeks later. Ewes give birth to lambs in a large "drop" pen. Sometimes, if the weather is nice, the ewes will have their lambs outside. Ewes almost always lamb on their own, without any assistance or interference from the shepherd. Most of the ewes give birth to twins or triplets, sometimes quadruplets.

The lambs are quick to get up and have their first meal. After a litter of lambs is born, they are put in a small pen (5 ft. x 5 ft.) called a "jug" with their dam (mother). Their navel cords are shortened, if necessary, and sprayed or dipped into a disinfectant, usually betadine. Being together in the jug helps the lambs and ewe bond and provides for easy observation by the shepherd. On the second day, the lambs are weighed, and ear tagged. The birth date, sex, weight, and ear tag number of each lamb is recorded. Lambs are sometimes docked or castrated. Docking is a common practice on farms where wooled breeds are raised.

Lambs will generally stay in the jugs for 1 to 3 days. After several days, the lambs and ewes are moved to mixing pens: Larger pens with approximately four ewes and their lambs. After being butted a few times by other ewes, the lambs quickly learn how to recognize their own mothers. Once they get used to each other, the lambs will huddle together to sleep and keep warm.

After a week or two in the mixing pens, groups of lambs and ewes are put with the rest of the ewes and their lambs. The lambs will be able to go anywhere in the barn. Ewes nursing triplet lambs are penned separately from ewes nursing twins because they receive extra grain to produce milk for their extra lamb.

By the time the lambs are two weeks old, they will have access to a creep area for creep feeding. A creep is a pen that is fenced so that young animals can enter but adults cannot. Creep feed is feed given to young nursing lambs. At most farms, the creep feed is a mixture of soybean meal and cracked corn. The lambs will also have access to fresh water, high quality hay, and minerals in the creep area. Even when they are not eating, the creep area is a place where the lambs like to hang out.

An Apt Comparison

The American Slave Coast: A History of the Slave-Breeding Industry by Ned and Constance Sublette is a book which offers an alternate view of slavery in the United States. Instead of treating slavery as a source of unpaid labor, as it is typically understood, they focus on the ownership aspect: People as property, merchandise, collateral, and capital.

Most American slaves were not kidnapped on another continent. Though over 12.7 million Africans were forced onto ships to be brought to the Western hemisphere, it is estimated that only 400,000-500,000 landed in present day America.

How then to account for the four million slaves who were tilling fields in 1860? "The South," the Sublettes write, "did not only produce tobacco, rice, sugar, and cotton as commodities for sale; it produced people." Slavers called slave breeding "natural increase," but there was nothing natural about producing slaves; it took scientific management. Thomas Jefferson bragged to George Washington that the birth of black children was increasing Virginia's capital stock by four percent annually.

This is how the American slave breeding industry worked, according to the Sublettes: Some states (most importantly Virginia) produced slaves as their main domestic output. The price of slaves was anchored by the industry of other states that consumed slaves in the production of rice and sugar, and constant territorial expansion.

As long as the slave power (i.e., America) continued to grow, breeders could literally bank on future demand and increasing prices. This made slaves not just a commodity, but the closest thing to money that a European American breeder had. It's hard to quantify just how valuable people were as commodities, but the Sublettes try: By conservative estimate, in 1860, the total value of American slaves was $4 billion, far more than the gold and silver then circulating nationally ($228.3 million, "most of it in the North"), total currency in circulation ($435.4 million), and even the value of the South's total farmland ($1.92 billion). Slaves were, to slavers, worth more than everything else they could imagine, combined.

The Sublettes also recast the 1808 abolition of the transatlantic slave trade as trade protectionism. Virginia slaveowners won a major victory when Thomas Jefferson's 1808 prohibition of African slave trade protected the domestic slave markets for slave breeding. By growing slave populations, southern states were literally manufacturing more political representation due to the Three-Fifths clause in the U.S. Constitution. They bred more slaves to help politically safeguard the practice of slavery.

Because slaves were property, Southern slave owners could mortgage them to banks and then the banks could package the mortgages into bonds and sell the bonds to anyone anywhere in the world, even where slavery was illegal.

In the 1830s, powerful Southern slaveowners wanted to import capital into their states so they could buy more slaves. They came up with a new, two-part idea: Mortgaging slaves, and then turning the mortgages into bonds that could be marketed all over the world. First, American planters organized new banks, usually in new states like Mississippi and Louisiana. Drawing up lists of slaves for collateral, the planters then mortgaged them to the banks they had created, enabling themselves to buy additional slaves to expand cotton production. To provide capital for those loans, the banks sold bonds to investors from around the globe, including in London, New York, Amsterdam, and Paris. The bond buyers, many of whom lived in countries where slavery was illegal, didn't own individual slaves, just these bonds backed by their value. Planters' mortgage payments paid the interest and the principle on these bond payments. Enslaved human beings had been, in modern financial lingo, "securitized," slave backed securities.

Tyler Cowen read *The American Slave Coast* and listed a few things he learned from it: President James Polk speculated in slaves, based on insider information he obtained from being President, and shaped American policy toward slaves and slave importation. In the South there were slave "breeding farms," where the number of women and children far outnumbered the number of men.

In his book *The Half Has Never Been Told: Slavery and the Making of American Capitalism*, historian Edward Baptist details how slavery played a central role in the making of the U.S. economy. As his book reveals, slavery and its expansion were central to the evolution and modernization of our nation in the 18th and 19th centuries, catapulting the U.S. into a modern, industrial, and capitalist economy. In the span of a single lifetime, the South grew from a narrow coastal strip of worn-out tobacco plantations to a sub-continental cotton empire.

CHAPTER 3

By 1861 it had five times as many slaves as it had during the Revolution and was producing two billion pounds of cotton a year. It was through slavery and slavery alone that the United States achieved a virtual monopoly on the production of cotton, the key raw material of the Industrial Revolution, and was transformed into a global power rivaled only by England.

Now you may ask, why do I use this sick comparison between sheep and slaves? The reason is plain: It's a fact. In America there was a breeding of human beings for profit, just as there was a breeding of sheep for profit.

Now let's make sure this is understood: Slavery has been around since the beginning of time, brutal slavery. As a matter of fact, the first slaves that were brought to America, otherwise known as indentured servants, were European Americans. They had to work seven years in America, and after the seven years, they would be given their own piece of land to own. This is something they weren't able to do where they were coming from, most being from an impoverished background.

However, these indentured servants ended up being more trouble than they were worth, as far as the wealthy plantation/landowners were concerned. Being able to read and write in English, they posed many legal problems simply by being familiar with the law. Also, a lot of them died before the seven years were finished, because they couldn't bare the harshness of the labor.

There were also slaves in North Africa itself. And it was soon discovered that these slaves were more profitable than indentured servants, when they became part of the American slave trade. They didn't know the English language or laws, they were already considered property (not indentured servants), so they could be treated like property, and they were considered slaves for life, as were their children. They and their children would die as slaves. Also, since they were coming from slavery, they were already used to being subservient.

Not Sheep, But Rams
I'm getting to the point here, so please be patient. I just have to lay some groundwork so the point will be completely understood.

Now since you've read this far, you should already know the answer to this question, but I'm going to ask anyway just in case you missed it at the beginning of the book: What do you call an adult male sheep? I did not know myself, and when I found out, it caught me by surprise because all I knew of sheep was what I saw on television. And as I said earlier, all I was shown on television were ewes (female sheep) and lambs (sheep less than one year old). I never saw the father/husband sheep, which is called a ram.

I thought that one of the ewes I saw was the adult male sheep, and I thought that all sheep were passive prey animals. But it turns out that what I and you have been witnessing on TV and elsewhere are sheep without their God ordained protector. Have you ever seen a ram? Rams are fierce. They name trucks after rams, the Dodge Ram. As a matter of fact, that's one of the ways I knew I was supposed to write this book. I had the unction to write a book based on rams, so I started researching them. At the same time, as I was researching, the Los Angeles Rams were in the playoffs, and I felt that if the Rams win the Superbowl, that would be my confirmation that God wanted me to write this book. So, congratulations to the Los Angeles Rams and here we are. The Rams are back!

CHAPTER 3

Farmers and breeders have dogs, llamas, donkeys, and even goats as guardians for their flock of sheep. With the rams in the picture, I don't think this would be necessary. So, what is the problem? Why are the rams not in the picture and only, as you noticed from our previous section, brought in for mating? From my research, I found that rams are hard to control. They fight each other to prove who is dominate and to see who will get the girl (ewe). They ram (headbutt) the gates and fences often, eventually tearing them down. They will fight the shepherd to protect the ewes and the lambs. For this reason, farmers and breeders have few rams on their property, if any. Some will just rent rams for breeding purposes. But even if they have rams, they are never kept with the ewes and the lambs.

So, for thousands of years, sheep have only known the rams as a tool for breeding, nothing more. Not a father, not a husband, not a protector, not a provider, just an instrument for mating. That's a sad way to see yourself, as well as to be seen. In this type of environment, where do your God-given instincts go? Your instinct to be a provider, a protector, a leader, a guide, a visionary, a father, and a husband? Even if you feel that you are supposed to be these things, but your environment negates the opportunity, what can you do? When no one sees you in this light, as a leader, as a father, what do you do? Some people become what everyone else sees them to be, or, even more, what they want you to think they see. In this way, you become what they need you to be to fulfill their agenda.

Sheep to the Slaughter

As it is written in Psalms 44:22/Romans 8:36: "For your sake we face death all day long; we are considered as sheep to be slaughtered."

Let me straighten out any misunderstanding this passage may cause. These scriptures are by no means saying that it is acceptable to God to treat human beings like animals. If you read the whole of Romans 8, you'll see that Paul said Jesus died for us, for our guilt, sin, and death. So, for His benefit, we die to our flesh that was crucified along with Him, daily. Every time you act in a way Jesus would, rather than the way your human nature wants you to, you are killing your flesh (your natural instinct, your human nature without the guidance of the Holy Spirit) and taking on the image of Christ.

Numbers 18:1-2a says, "So the Lord said to Aaron, 'You and your sons and your father's household (family) with you shall bear the guilt in connection with the sanctuary [that is, through your service as priests you will atone for the offenses which the people unknowingly commit when brought into contact with the manifestations of God's presence].'" This is a foreshadowing of Jesus' position as High Priest, seated at the right hand of the Father in Heaven, interceding on our behalf.

If you read Psalms chapters 44 and 45, you'll see the foreshadowing of the life, crucifixion, death, resurrection, and reign of Jesus Christ and His Bride. In 44:1-8 we see Jesus' walking in His calling, walking in victory and in the purpose and direction of God the Father. In 44:9-16 we see Jesus' suffering on the day of His crucifixion. It is in 44:17-26 when Jesus died. In 45:1-8, Jesus Reigns. In 45:9-17, The Bride of Christ (us) Reigns with Him. In Matthew 12:38-40, some of the scribes

CHAPTER 3

and pharisees said to Jesus, "Teacher we want to see a sign (attesting miracle) from You (proving that You are what You claim to be)." But Jesus told them the only sign they would see was the sign of the prophet Jonah. "For just as Jonah was in the belly of the whale for three days and three nights, so will the Son of Man be three days and three nights in the heart of the earth." Some people say Jonah was alive in the whale, but that goes against what Jesus is saying, because we know Jesus died on the cross, was buried dead, stayed dead for 3 days and 3 nights, and rose with all power in His hands. This is as Jonah was vomited out of the mouth of the whale after 3 days and 3 nights.

Jesus humbled himself before the Father and sacrificed His life for the whole world. Not just mankind, but for all life. Romans 8:1-39 says,

> "Therefore there is now no condemnation [no guilty verdict, no punishment] for those who are in Christ Jesus [who believe in Him as personal Lord and Savior]. For the law of the Spirit of life [which is] in Christ Jesus [the law of our new being] has set you free from the law of sin and of death. For what the Law could not do [that is, overcome sin and remove its penalty, its power] being weakened by the flesh [man's nature without the Holy Spirit], God did: He sent His own Son in the likeness of sinful man as an offering for sin. And He condemned sin in the flesh [subdued it and overcame it in the person of His own Son], so that the [righteous and just] requirement of the Law might be fulfilled in us who do not live our lives in the ways of the flesh [guided by worldliness and our sinful nature], but [live our lives] in the ways of the Spirit [guided by His power].

"For those who are living according to the flesh set their minds on the things of the flesh [which gratify the body], but those who are living according to the Spirit, [set their minds on] the things of the Spirit [His will and purpose]. Now the mind of the flesh is death [both now and forever because it pursues sin]; but the mind of the Spirit is life and peace [the spiritual well-being that comes from walking with God both now and forever]; the mind of the flesh [with its sinful pursuits] is actively hostile to God.

"It does not submit itself to God's law, since it cannot, and those who are in the flesh [living a life that caters to sinful appetites and impulses] cannot please God. However, you are not [living] in the flesh [controlled by the sinful nature] but in the Spirit, if in fact the Spirit of God lives in you [directing and guiding you]. But if anyone does not have the Spirit of Christ, he does not belong to Him [and is not a child of God]. If Christ lives in you, though your [natural] body is dead because of sin, your spirit is alive because of righteousness [which He provides]. And if the Spirit of Him who raised Jesus from the dead lives in you, He who raised Christ Jesus from the dead will also give life to your mortal bodies through His Spirit, who lives in you. So then, brothers and sisters, we have an obligation, but not to our flesh [our human nature, our worldliness, our sinful capacity], to live according to the [impulses of the] flesh [our nature without the Holy Spirit] for if you are living according to the [impulses of the] flesh, you are going to die (be separated from God).

"But if [you are living] by the [power of the Holy] Spirit you are habitually putting to death the sinful deeds of the body, you will [really] live forever (eternal life). For all who are allowing themselves *to* be led by the Spirit of God are sons of God. For you have not received a spirit of slavery leading again to fear [of God's judgment], but you have received the Spirit of adoption as sons [the Spirit producing sonship] by which we [joyfully] cry, 'Abba! Father!'

"The Spirit Himself testifies and confirms together with our spirit [assuring us] that we [believers] are children of God. And if [we are His] children, [then we are His] heirs also: heirs of God and fellow heirs with Christ [sharing His spiritual blessing and inheritance], if indeed we share in His suffering so that we may also share in His glory.

"For I consider [from the standpoint of faith] that the sufferings of the present life are not worthy to be compared with the glory that is about to be revealed to us and in us! For [even the whole] creation [all nature] waits eagerly for the children of God to be revealed. For the creation was subjected to frustration and futility, not willingly [because of some intentional fault on its part], but by the will of Him who subjected it, in hope that the creation itself will also be freed from its bondage to decay [and gain entrance] into the glorious freedom of the children of God. For we know that the whole creation has been moaning together as in the pains of childbirth until now. And not only this, but we too, who have the first fruits of the Spirit [a joyful indication of the blessings to come], even we groan inwardly, as we wait eagerly for [the sign of] our adoption as sons, the redemption and transformation of our body [at the resurrection].

"For in this hope, we were saved [by faith]. But hope [the object of] which is seen is not hope. For who hopes for what he already sees? But if we hope for what we do not see, we wait eagerly for it with patience and composure. In the same way the Spirit [comes to us and] helps us in our weakness. We do not know what prayer to offer or how to offer it as we should, but the Spirit Himself [knows our need and at the right time] intercedes on our behalf with sighs and groanings too deep for words. And He who searches the hearts knows what the mind of the Spirit is, because the Spirit intercedes [before God] on behalf of God's people in accordance with God's will. And we know [with great confidence] that God [who is deeply concerned about us] causes all things to work together [as a plan] for good for those who love God, to those who are called according to His plan and purpose.

"For those whom He foreknew [and loved and chose beforehand], He also predestined to be conformed to the image of His Son [and ultimately share in His complete sanctification], so that He would be the firstborn [the most beloved and honored] among many believers. And those whom He predestined, He also called; and those whom He called, He also justified [declared free of the guilt of sin]; and those whom He justified, He also glorified [raising them to a heavenly dignity]. What then shall we say to all these things? If God is for us, who can be [successful] against us? He who did not spare [even] His own Son, but gave Him up for us all, how will He not also, along with Him, graciously give us all things? Who will bring any charge against God's elect (His chosen ones)? It is God who justifies us [declaring us blameless and putting us in a right relationship with Himself]. Who is the one who condemns us? Christ Jesus is the One who died [to pay our penalty], and more than that, who was raised [from the dead], and who is at the right hand of God interceding [with the Father] for us. Who shall ever separate us from the love of Christ? Will tribulation, or distress, or persecution, or famine, or nakedness, or danger, or sword? Just as it is written and forever remains written,

"For Your sake we are put to death all day long;
We are regarded as sheep for the slaughter.

"Yet in all these things we are more than conquerors and gain an overwhelming victory through Him who loved us [so much that He died for us]. For I am convinced [and continue to be convinced beyond any doubt] that neither death, nor life, nor angels, nor principalities, nor things present and threatening, nor things to come, nor powers, nor height, nor depth, nor any other created thing, will be able to separate us from the [unlimited] love of God, which is in Christ Jesus our Lord."

All of creation, the whole world, Earth, the universe, and everything in them, has been eagerly waiting for the Children of God to get their act together. I hear people say they believe in the universe. That's one of the problems with the world today. We're so set on not believing in God until we're willing to believe in the power of the very things God has given us the power and authority to manage. The universe, earth, moon, and stars are waiting for us to finally take on the true God-given authority and purpose of our lives and we are instead bowing down to them, because we don't know who we are in Christ.

These very things will testify against us. Because they had nothing to do with us bowing down and worshipping them. They were just being as amazing as God created them to be. Our refusal to believe in God has pushed us to worship the awesomeness of His creation. Romans 1:20 says, "For ever since the creation of the world His invisible attributes, His eternal power and divine nature, have been clearly seen, being understood through His workmanship [all His creation, the wonderful things that He has made], so that they [who fail to believe and trust in Him] are without excuse and without defense."

Our God-Given Purpose
Okay, you may say, then what is our God-given purpose? What is it that all of creation is waiting on? Easy! (Though we've prayed it so much they've become mere words.) "Our Father, who is in Heaven, Holy is your name. YOUR KINGDOM COME; YOUR WILL BE DONE ON EARTH AS IT IS IN HEAVEN." Our purpose is to usher The Manifest Glory of God into every area of life. The world is to be saturated with the presence (Glory) of God. Not the presence of religion, but the Manifest Presence (Glory) of God.

Psalms 110:1-4 says,

"The Lord (Father) says to my Lord (the Messiah, His Son), 'Sit at My right hand
Until I make Your enemies a footstool for Your feet [subjugating them into complete submission].'
The Lord will send the scepter of Your strength from Zion, saying, 'Rule in the midst of Your enemies.'
Your people will offer themselves willingly [to participate in Your battle] in the day of Your power;
In the splendor of holiness, from the womb of the dawn, Your young men are to You as the dew. The Lord has sworn [an oath] and will not change His mind: 'You are a priest forever According to the order of Melchizedek.'"

Daniel 7:13-14 says,

"I kept looking in the night visions, and behold, on the clouds of heaven One like a Son of Man was coming, and He came up to the Ancient of Days and was presented before Him. And to Him (the Messiah) was given dominion (supreme authority), Glory and a kingdom, that all the peoples, nations, and speakers of every language Should serve and worship Him. His dominion is an everlasting dominion Which will not pass away; And His kingdom is one Which will not be destroyed."

Revelation 12:7-12 says,

"And war broke out in heaven, Michael [the archangel] and his angels waging war with the dragon. The dragon and his angels fought, but they were not strong enough and did not prevail, and there was no longer a place found for them in heaven. And the great dragon was thrown down, the age-old serpent who is called the devil and Satan, he who continually deceives and seduces the entire inhabited world; he was thrown down to the earth, and his angels were thrown down with him.

"Then I heard a loud voice in heaven, saying, 'Now the salvation, and the power, and the kingdom (dominion, reign) of our God, and the authority of His Christ have come; for the accuser of our [believing] brothers and sisters has been thrown down [at last], he who accuses them and keeps bringing charges [of sinful behavior] against them before our God day and night. And they overcame and conquered him because of the blood of the Lamb and because of the word of their testimony, for they did not love their life and renounce their faith even when faced with death (separation from God). Therefore rejoice, O heavens and you who dwell in them [in the presence of God]. Woe to the earth and the sea, because the devil has come down to you in great wrath, knowing that he has only a short time [remaining]!'"

As I read Revelations 12:7-12, it tells me that war was waged in heaven and Satan and his angels were defeated. Or better said, Satan and God's angels who were deceived by Satan were defeated. As I continued to read, I noticed that Satan was accusing and bringing charges (of sinful behavior) against the inhabitants of heaven to God, day and night. And those in heaven overcame and conquered Satan because of the blood of the Lamb and because of the word of their testimony, for they did not love their life and renounce their faith even when faced with death (separation from God). "Therefore rejoice, O heavens and you who dwell in them (in the presence of God). Woe to the earth and the sea, because the devil has come down to you in great wrath, knowing that he has only a short time (remaining)!"

Satan is now trying to raise another army, this time an earthy army, a human army to wage another war against God.

In Matthew 24:9-12 Jesus says,

"Be careful that no one misleads you [deceiving you and leading you into error]. For many will come in My name [misusing it and appropriating the strength of the name which belongs to Me], saying, 'I am the Christ (the Messiah, the Anointed),' and they will mislead many. You will continually hear of wars and rumors of wars. See that you are not frightened, for those things must take place, but that is not yet the end [of the age]. For nation will rise against nation, and kingdom against kingdom, and there will be famines and earthquakes in various places.

"'But all these things are merely the beginning of birth pangs [of the intolerable anguish and the time of unprecedented trouble]. Then they will hand you over to [endure] tribulation, and will put you to death, and you will be hated by all nations because of My name. At that time many will be offended and repelled [by their association with Me] and will fall away [from the One whom they should trust] and will betray one another [handing over believers to their persecutors] and will hate one another. Many false prophets will appear and mislead many. Because lawlessness is increased, the love of most people will grow cold. But the one who endures and bears up [under suffering] to the end will be saved. This good news of the kingdom [the gospel] will be preached throughout the whole world as a testimony to all the nations, and then the end [of the age] will come.'"

John 18:35-36 says,

"Pilate answered, "'I am not a Jew, am I? Your own people and their chief priests have handed You over to me. What have You done [that is worthy of death]?' Jesus replied, 'My kingdom is not of this world [nor does it have its origin in this world]. If My kingdom were of this world, My servants would be fighting [hard] to keep Me from being handed over to the Jews; but as it is, My kingdom is not of this world.'"

John 4:23-24 says,

"But a time is coming and is already here when the true worshipers will worship the Father in spirit [from the heart, the inner self] and in truth; for the Father seeks such people to be His worshipers. God is spirit [the Source of life, yet invisible to mankind], and those who worship Him must worship in spirit and truth."

2 Corinthians 10:3-6 says,

"For though we walk in the flesh [as mortal men], we are not carrying on our [spiritual] warfare according to the flesh and using the weapons of man. The weapons of our warfare are not physical [weapons of flesh and blood]. Our weapons are divinely powerful for the destruction of fortresses. We are destroying sophisticated arguments and every exalted and proud thing that sets itself up against the [true] knowledge of God, and we are taking every thought and purpose captive to the obedience of Christ, being ready to punish every act of disobedience, when your own obedience [as a church, The Body of Christ] is complete. You are looking [only] at the outward appearance of things. If anyone is confident that he is Christ's, he should reflect and consider this, that just as he is Christ's, so too are we."

In Genesis 12:3 God gives Abram (Abraham) a promise:

"And I will bless (do good for, benefit) those who bless you, And I will curse [that is, subject to My wrath and judgment] the one who curses (despises, dishonors, has contempt for) you. And in you all the families (nations) of the earth will be blessed."

They Know Not What They Do

Now what really caught my attention in this scripture was the fact that God said, "I will bless those who bless you and I will curse the one who curses you." I went to the King James Version, and it says, "I will curse him who curses you," singular. The fight is not with each other. That's why God is so keen on forgiveness. That's why Jesus said, "forgive them Father, for they know not what they do." Satan has been given the dust (man without the spirit of God, flesh, carnal nature) to rule and control. If we try to fight Satan without God, we will lose as we have been doing.

You might say, "I'm not losing, I'm winning! I have everything I could ever want in this world and then some." But you are selfish and greedy. YOU ARE LOSING! Success is not about what or how much you obtain in this world, it's about whether you fulfilled your God-given purpose while you were in this world. Because that, that purpose, is what will last; it is eternal.

Everything else is left here. Everything else will one day decay and die. The money, the fame, the fortune, the accolades, everything. You can obtain all of the money in the world and leave the world in ruins, if your mission was to make money at any cost. God's Mission (Advancement of the Kingdom of God) will cause the whole world to thrive.

You might notice that the more mankind goes up, the more the world goes down. This is because mankind is not following the instructions of God and in our own prideful mind we are just taking care of business. We are not understanding that there are only two influences in this world: God and Satan. You're following the design of one or the other, and if you haven't made a conscious choice to follow God, more than likely your decisions are influenced by Satan.

Just look at the direction the world is going in. When new things begin, it's like "wow what a discovery," but as time goes by we see that those discoveries end up sucking the life out of the whole world and everyone in it.

There's a passage in the Bible that says, "there's a way that seems right to a man, but the end is destruction." God's design will preserve life and cause things to flourish and blossom forever. If your design starts out good and ends badly for everyone, including yourself, check the true manufacturer. Hint: It's not you (it's Satan). The Bible says "No one can serve two masters; for either he will hate the one and love the other, or he will be devoted to the one and despise the other. You cannot serve God and mammon (money, possessions, fame, status, or whatever is valued more than the Lord)." Why? The answer is in one word: Serve!

Matthew 6:33 says,

> "But first and most importantly seek (aim at, strive after) The Kingdom of God and His righteousness (His way of doing and being right, the attitude and character of God), and all these things will be given to you also." If you seek money without acknowledging God, you will lose God, but if you seek God, truly seek God, not religion, money will hunt you down.

Now this is where a problem could come in, and if this is the case you first need deliverance (God's divine help) with this. Ecclesiastes 5:10-17 says,

> "He who loves money will not be satisfied with money, nor he who loves abundance with its gain.

This too is vanity (emptiness). When good things increase, those who consume them increase. So what advantage is there to their owners except to see them with their eyes? The sleep of a working man is sweet, whether he eats little or much; but the full stomach (greed) of the rich [who hungers for even more] will not let him sleep."

1 Timothy 6:10 says,

"For the love of money is a root of all kinds of evil. Some people, eager for money, have wandered from the faith and pierced themselves with many griefs. Now the Bible doesn't say money is evil, money is neither good nor bad, it depends on the person who's hand it's in that makes that determination. Money can be the best thing in the world and help in the saving and betterment of the world or money can be the root cause of mass destruction. It all depends on how we, as a whole, use it and the position we place it in, in our lives. How much damage has been done to the world and those in it for the love of money? How much have we lost collectively and individually for the love of money? Not because of money. Money makes no decisions, but the position we've given money is the position only God should have (Supreme Authority)."

Ecclesiastes 10:19 says,

"A feast is made for laughter, wine makes life merry, and money is the answer for everything. Money was created by God. It doesn't matter what man He gave the idea to, to answer everything we would ever need answered. The question of homelessness, poverty, sickness and disease. But mankind's love for what money could do caused mankind to worship (show the importance or value of someone or something) money. Putting money before any and everything including God."

"There is a grievous evil which I have seen under the sun: riches being kept and hoarded by their owner to his own misery. For when those riches are lost in bad investments and he becomes the father of a son, then there is nothing in his hand [for the support of the child]. As he came naked from his mother's womb, so he will return as he came; and he will take away nothing from all his labor that he can carry in his hand. This also is a grievous evil, exactly as he was born, so he shall die.

"So, what advantage has he who labors for the wind? All of his life he also eats in darkness [cheerlessly, without sweetness and light], with great frustration, sickness, and anger. Behold, here is what I have seen to be good and fitting: to eat and drink, and to find enjoyment in all the labor in which he labors under the sun during the few days of his life which God gives him, for this is his [allotted] reward. Also, every man to whom God has given riches and possessions, He has also given the power and ability to enjoy them and to receive [this as] his [allotted] portion and to rejoice in his labor, this is the gift of God [to him]. For he will not often consider the [troubled] days of his life, because God keeps him occupied and focused on the joy of his heart [and the tranquility of God indwells him]."

There is a definite difference between the man who serves money and becomes wealthy and the man who serves God and becomes wealthy. But the thing you have to be willing to accept is that you are not to seek money. You are to seek ways to promote God's Kingdom and this in turn links you to wealth.

There is a scripture about a rich young ruler. Luke 18:18-30 says,

> "A certain ruler asked Jesus, 'Good Teacher [You who are essentially and morally good], what shall I do to inherit eternal life [that is, eternal salvation in the Messiah's kingdom, The Kingdom of God]?' Jesus said to him, 'Why do you call Me good? No one is [essentially and morally] good except God alone. You know the commandments: "Do not commit adultery, do not murder, do not steal, do not testify falsely, Honor your father and your mother."' He replied, 'I have kept all these things from my youth.' When Jesus heard this, He said to him, 'You still lack one thing; sell everything that you have and distribute the money to the poor, and you will have [abundant] treasure in heaven; and come, follow Me [becoming My disciple, believing and trusting in Me and walking the same path of life that I walk].'

> "But when he heard these things, he became very sad, for he was extremely rich. Jesus looked at him and said, 'How difficult it is for those who are wealthy to enter the kingdom of God! For it is easier for a camel to go through the eye of a needle than for a rich man [who places his faith in wealth or status] to enter the kingdom of God.' And those who heard it said, 'Then who can be saved?' But He said, 'The things that are impossible with people are possible with God.' Peter said, 'Look, we have left all [things, homes, families, businesses] and followed You.' And He said to them, 'I assure you and most solemnly say to you, there is no

one who has left house or wife or brothers or parents or children for the sake of the kingdom of God, who will not receive many times as much in this present age and in the age to come, eternal life.'"

The question is, why is it so hard for the wealthy to enter the Kingdom of God? Ecclesiastes 10:19 says, "The officials make a feast for enjoyment [instead of repairing what is broken], and serve wine to make life merry, and money is the answer to everything."

Money is the answer to everything on earth, so when you have the answer to what you believe to be everything, without an in-depth God-ordained answer to why you should, it's going to be hard to give it up. So, what Jesus was telling the rich young ruler is, money is your God and the reason I know it, is because after talking to God (Jesus Christ) the rich young ruler became sad because he realized what Jesus said was true. Anything you can't give up for God has become your god.

So, what do you do when you know you must change, but you realize you don't have the power or strength within you to make what would seem to be such a drastic change? You ask God to help you. You be honest with yourself, because God already knows, and you say, God I can't do this on my own, this is all I know, this is the only way I know how to be, I've trusted and relied on this way of life for as long as I can remember, my whole life. My parents, and their parents, relied on this way of life. I wouldn't know how to change if I wanted to, and I do want to, but I just can't see how it's possible. My whole life, my very being is connected to this way of life, this lifestyle. What do you want me to do?

The last question is all God needs. He knew about everything you felt you needed to tell Him before He called you and believe and understand this is a call. And if you're willing to answer, God through His Holy Spirit will show you the way. He will help you, lead you, and guide you into all righteousness (right standing with God). He is the only way; it's impossible for you to do this on your own. And God has made it that way because He wants to build a relationship with you. GOD LOVES YOU!!!

John 19:10-11 says,

> "So, Pilate said to Jesus, 'You do not speak to me? Do You not know that I have authority to release You, and I have authority to crucify You?' Jesus answered, 'You would have no authority over Me at all if it had not been given to you from above. For this reason, the sin and guilt of the one who handed Me over to you is greater [than your own].'"

This is what is widely misunderstood: All authority, power, wealth, and riches have been allowed by God. So, whether you are using what God has allowed you to have for His purpose or not, somehow God is getting or going to get the Glory out of it. No one has anything that God didn't allow them to have for whatever His reason. Jesus tells Pilate, you're just doing what My Father (God) gave you the authority to do, administer justice, but the person who turned me over to you did not operate in their designed calling, speaking of Judas Iscariot. Judas was called to be an Apostle, but he chose to be a traitor.

John 17:1-26 says,

> "When Jesus had spoken these things, He raised His eyes to heaven [in prayer] and said, 'Father, the hour has come. Glorify Your Son, so that Your Son may

glorify You. Just as You have given Him power and authority over all mankind, [now glorify Him] so that He may give eternal life to all whom You have given Him [to be His permanently and forever]. Now this is eternal life: that they may know You, the only true [supreme and sovereign] God, and [in the same manner know] Jesus [as the] Christ whom You have sent. I have glorified You [down here] on the earth by completing the work that You gave Me to do.

"'Now, Father, glorify Me together with Yourself, with the glory and majesty that I had with You before the world existed. I have manifested Your name [and revealed Your very self, Your real self] to the people whom You have given Me out of the world; they were Yours and You gave them to Me, and they have kept and obeyed Your word. Now [at last] they know [with confident assurance] that all You have given Me is from You [it is really and truly Yours]. For the words which You gave Me I have given them; and they received and accepted them and truly understood [with confident assurance] that I came from You [from Your presence], and they believed [without any doubt] that You sent Me. I pray for them; I do not pray for the world, but for those You have given Me, because they belong to You; and all things that are Mine are Yours, and [all things that are] Yours are Mine; and I am glorified in them.

"'I am no longer in the world; yet they are still in the world, and I am coming to You. Holy Father, keep them in Your name, the name which You have given Me, so that they may be one just as We are. While I was with them, I was keeping them in Your name which You have given Me; and I guarded them and protected them, and not one of them was lost except the son of destruction, so that the Scripture would be fulfilled.

"'But now I am coming to You; and I say these things [while I am still] in the world so that they may experience My joy made full and complete and perfect within them [filling their hearts with My delight]. I have given to them Your word [the message You gave Me]; and the world has hated them because they are not of the world and do not belong to the world, just as I am not of the world and do not belong to it. I do not ask You to take them out of the world, but that You keep them and protect them from the evil one. They are not of the world, just as I am not of the world. Sanctify them in the truth [set them apart for Your purposes, make them holy]; Your word is truth.

"'Just as You commissioned and sent Me into the world, I also have commissioned and sent them (believers) into the world. For their sake I sanctify Myself [to do Your will], so that they also may be sanctified [set apart, dedicated, made holy] in [Your] truth. I do not pray for these alone [it is not for their sake only that I make this request], but also for [all] those who [will ever] believe and trust in Me through their message, that they all may be one; just as You, Father, are in Me and I in You, that they also may be one in Us, so that the world may believe [without any doubt] that You sent Me. I have given to them the glory and honor which You have given Me, that they may be one, just as We are one; I in them and You in Me, that they may be perfected and completed into one, so that the world may know [without any doubt] that You sent Me, and [that You] have loved them, just as You have loved Me.

"'Father, I desire that they also, whom You have given to Me [as Your gift to Me], may be with Me where I am, so that they may see My glory which You have given Me, because You loved Me before the foundation of the world. O just and righteous Father, although the world has not known You and has never acknowledged You [and the revelation of Your mercy], yet I have always known You; and these [believers] know [without any doubt] that You sent Me; and I have made Your name known to them, and will continue to make it known, so that the love with which You have loved Me may be in them [overwhelming their heart], and I [may be] in them.'"

Matthew 28:16-20 says,

"Now the eleven disciples went to Galilee, to the mountain which Jesus had designated. And when they saw Him, they worshiped Him; but some doubted [that it was really He]. Jesus came up and said to them, 'All authority (all power of absolute rule) in heaven and on earth has been given to Me. Go therefore and make disciples of all the nations [help the people to learn of Me, believe in Me, and obey My words], baptizing them in the name of the Father and of the Son and of the Holy Spirit, teaching them to observe everything that I have commanded you; and lo, I am with you always [remaining with you perpetually, regardless of circumstance, and on every occasion], even to the end of the age."

A True Citizen of the United States

Psalms 44:22/Romans 8:36 says, as it is written: "For your sake we face death all day long; we are considered as sheep to be slaughtered."

As Jesus (God) sends us out into the world (our families, our jobs, our community, our nation, the world), we understand that God doesn't want us to operate according to the situation or circumstances. We can operate that way if we want to, but it won't be according to God's will. Let me explain it this way. Now, I know some won't agree, but I'm going to explain it this way anyway. I believe God used both Martin Luther King Jr. and Malcolm X at the same time on purpose. And before you get your thoughts twisted, remember God is in control of everything and every person. In the end, it will all work out for God's Glory!

So, let me start with something we all need to know inside and out: The Declaration of Independence and the United States Constitution. I'm as guilty as anyone of not giving them the attention they deserve nor the understanding required to be a true citizen of the United States of America. There is a lot of complaining about what is going on in our nation. But have we taken the time to find out how it got this way or why it seems so difficult for things to change? If you read about how our nation started and begin to understand how our nation was freed from the control of Great Britain, you will start to get the picture.

Yes, at one time America was under the rule and authority of Great Britain. But our founding fathers did not feel that any person should have power, control, and authority over another human being. Which as the Bible tells us is exactly right. Galatians 3:26-29 says,

> "For you [who are born-again have been reborn from above spiritually transformed, renewed, sanctified and] are all children of God [set apart for His purpose with full rights and privileges] through faith in Christ

Jesus. For all of you who were baptized into Christ [into a spiritual union with the Christ, the Anointed] have clothed yourselves with Christ [that is, you have taken on His characteristics and values]. There is [now no distinction in regard to salvation] neither Jew nor Greek, there is neither slave nor free, there is neither male nor female; for you [who believe] are all one in Christ Jesus [no one can claim a spiritual superiority]. And if you belong to Christ [if you are in Him], then you are Abraham's descendants, and [spiritual] heirs according to [God's] promise."

But at the same time that our founding fathers were giving their passionate statements against inequality, they themselves were usurping power, control, and authority over other human beings. Yes, even Thomas Jefferson did so, who wrote in the Declaration of Independence:

"We hold these truths to be self-evident, that all men are created equal, that they are endowed by their Creator with certain unalienable Rights, that among these are Life, Liberty and the pursuit of Happiness."

Yes, even George Washington, whom I was taught in school sat under an apple tree and could not tell a lie, owned other human beings (slaves) at the same time he helped write the Declaration (The formal announcement of the beginning of a state or condition) of Independence (freedom from outside control; not depending on another's authority nor depending on another for livelihood or subsistence).

Two of the greatest documents given by our founding fathers were the Declaration of Independence and the United States Constitution. People across the religious spectrum, from the most devout believers to the most committed atheists, look to these documents for support. Yet their vision, mission, and purpose seem to have a different foundation. The Declaration of Independence is saturated with acknowledgment of God and our position in Him as human beings (Children of God). All of us! But the Declaration of Independence was written while America was under the rule and authority of Great Britain. The Declaration of Independence was written to give the reason why not just those in America, but why no one, should be subject to anyone else and denied the unalienable Rights that they have been endowed with by the Creator (God).

In contrast, the United States Constitution was written by the founding fathers after America had been freed from the rule and authority of Great Britain. Isn't it strange how things change when we get what we're asking for? There is not one mention of God in the United States Constitution. Why is this? Is it that our founding fathers never were concerned with God or His Will and just used His Name, Power, and Authority as a way to get free from bondage? I hope not! Is it that they felt they no longer needed God's influence since they already got what they wanted? I sure hope not!

The idea I'm leaning toward is that they didn't know how to both implement God and live the way they wanted to live and operate the way they wanted to operate as a Country. See, it's easy to cry out to God when you are down and can't see any other way, but it's hard to do what you promised God you would do after He gives you the strength you need to get up. Every college student remembers that one time when they were face down in the toilet and told God, "God forgive me, if you keep me from dying, I will never do this again" and you kept your promise, until your hangover was gone, and your stomach started to feel better. Lol. That joke was not for the Super Saints. You won't understand that one. That's for those Saints like me, who don't even understand why, after all you've done, after all you've put God through, God would even let you look at His Kingdom, much less give you a job in it. But Super Brothers and Sisters keep reading, I'll have a joke for you, as well. Lol. I Love You'll!!!

This one is for my Super Brother and Sisters, to help you understand what was going on between America and Great Britain. The Declaration of Independence asserted the purpose of the American government, the Colonists grievances with British rule, and signaled the newly formed country's intention to fight for democracy and self-rule.

It's a lot like this:

Dear Mom and Dad,

Two days ago, I made a very important decision. I've got a right to be happy and to live my own life, my own way. So, I am writing you this letter to let you know I don't want you to interfere in my life anymore. For the last few years, you've been taking advantage of me and treating me like a child with your unfair rules, and I'm not going to take it anymore! You say no to every reasonable request I make, and you don't give me any privacy. You won't let me pick my own job, you won't listen to my side of the story, and whenever I try to do something for myself, you say I'm being rebellious. But you keep changing the rules and you won't talk to me, so how am I supposed to know what you expect? You know I've tried to fix the problems between us, but you just won't listen. So,

CHAPTER 3

I'm done. I'm moving out, and I no longer consider you, my parents.

Sincerely,
Your former daughter

On July 4, 1776, the Second Continental Congress sent off a letter just like that one. They told King George III that since he refused to respect their rights as British citizens, they were going to disown him. Today, we know this letter as the Declaration of Independence.

Tensions had been escalating between the colonies and the British government since the end of the French and Indian War in 1763. Sustained warfare broke out 12 years later, in 1775. At the beginning of the war, very few people on either side of the Atlantic thought this was a war for independence. The colonist's original goal had been to fight for the rights to which they felt they were entitled. Public opinion shifted in favor of independence following the publication of *Common Sense* in January 1776. And it was the King's reaction to the colonists Olive Branch Petition and continued military action by the British that finally convinced the colonial leaders that the best course of action was to break completely with Great Britain and try to make it in the world on their own.

In May 1776, the Congress endorsed overthrowing the existing royal governments. Every colony that did not yet have a Patriot government established one, and they began calling themselves states. In June, a committee of five congressmen led by Thomas Jefferson met to draft the Declaration of Independence. On July 2, 1776, the Continental Congress voted in favor of independence, though not unanimously. Benjamin Franklin famously encouraged all of the delegates to vote in favor of independence by saying "We must all hang together, or assuredly we shall all hang separately."

But there were some disagreements about the wording of the document. In particular, many delegates were disturbed by the declaration's mention of slavery. Jefferson himself owned hundreds of slaves, but still, the first draft of the Declaration of Independence blamed the King for "maintaining a market where men are bought and sold." Since South Carolina and Georgia refused to accept it as it stood, the Declaration was amended to ignore slavery before it was signed by Congress. So, on the fourth of July, Congress approved the wording of the formal declaration, and John Hancock, president of the Congress, signed it.

CHAPTER 4

The Declaration of Independence and The U.S. Constitution

The Declaration of Independence

"When in the Course of human events, it becomes necessary for one people to dissolve the political bands which have connected them with another, and to assume among the powers of the earth, the separate and equal station to which the Laws of Nature and of Nature's God entitle them, a decent respect to the opinions of mankind requires that they should declare the causes which impel them to the separation.

"We hold these truths to be self-evident, that all men are created equal, that they are endowed by their Creator with certain unalienable Rights, that among these are Life, Liberty and the pursuit of Happiness. That to secure these rights, Governments are instituted among Men, deriving their just powers from the consent of the governed, that whenever any Form of Government becomes destructive of these ends, it is the Right of the People to alter or to abolish it, and to institute new Government, laying its foundation on such principles and organizing its powers in such form, as to them shall seem most likely to affect their Safety and Happiness. Prudence, indeed, will dictate that Governments long established should not be changed for light and transient causes; and accordingly, all experience hath shewn, that mankind is more disposed to suffer, while evils are sufferable, than to right themselves by abolishing the forms to which they are accustomed. But when a long train of abuses and usurpations, pursuing invariably the same Object evinces a design to reduce them under absolute Despotism, it is their right, it is their duty, to throw off such Government, and to provide new Guards for their future security. Such has been the patient sufferance of these Colonies; and such is now the necessity which constrains them to alter their former Systems of Government. The history of the present King of Great Britain is a history of repeated injuries and usurpations, all having in direct object the establishment of an absolute Tyranny over these States. To prove this, let Facts be submitted to a candid world.

"He has refused his Assent to Laws, the most wholesome and necessary for the public good.

"He has forbidden his Governors to pass Laws of immediate and pressing importance, unless suspended in their operation till his Assent should be obtained; and when so suspended, he has utterly neglected to attend to them.

"He has refused to pass other Laws for the accommodation of large districts of people, unless those people would relinquish the right of Representation in the Legislature, a right inestimable to them and formidable to tyrants only.

"He has called together legislative bodies at places unusual, uncomfortable, and distant from the depository of their public Records, for the sole purpose of fatiguing them into compliance with his measures.

"He has dissolved Representative Houses repeatedly, for opposing with manly firmness his invasions on the rights of the people.

"He has refused for a long time, after such dissolutions, to cause others to be elected; whereby the Legislative powers, incapable of Annihilation, have returned to the People at large for their exercise; the State remaining in the meantime exposed to all the dangers of invasion from without, and convulsions within.

"He has endeavored to prevent the population of these States; for that purpose, obstructing the Laws for Naturalization of Foreigners; refusing to pass others to encourage their migrations hither, and raising the conditions of new Appropriations of Lands.

"He has obstructed the Administration of Justice, by refusing his Assent to Laws for establishing Judiciary powers.

"He has made Judges dependent on his Will alone, for the tenure of their offices, and the amount and payment of their salaries.

"He has erected a multitude of New Offices and sent hither swarms of Officers to harrass our people and eat out their substance.

"He has kept among us, in times of peace, Standing Armies without the Consent of our legislatures.

"He has affected to render the Military independent of and superior to the Civil power.

"He has combined with others to subject us to a jurisdiction foreign to our constitution, and unacknowledged by our laws, giving his Assent to their Acts of pretended Legislation:

"For Quartering large bodies of armed troops among us:

"For protecting them, by a mock Trial, from punishment for any Murders which they should commit on the Inhabitants of these States:

"For cutting off our Trade with all parts of the world:

"For imposing Taxes on us without our Consent:

"For depriving us in many cases, of the benefits of Trial by Jury:

"For transporting us beyond Seas to be tried for pretended offences

"For abolishing the free System of English Laws in a neighboring Province, establishing therein an Arbitrary government, and enlarging its Boundaries so as to render it at once an example and fit instrument for introducing the same absolute rule into these Colonies:

"For taking away our Charters, abolishing our most valuable Laws, and altering fundamentally the Forms of our Governments:

"For suspending our own Legislatures and declaring themselves invested with power to legislate for us in all cases whatsoever.

"He has abdicated Government here, by declaring us out of his Protection and waging War against us.

"He has plundered our seas, ravaged our Coasts, burnt our towns, and destroyed the lives of our people.

"He is at this time transporting large Armies of foreign Mercenaries to complete the works of death, desolation and tyranny, already begun with circumstances of Cruelty & perfidy scarcely paralleled in the most barbarous ages, and totally unworthy the Head of a civilized nation.

"He has constrained our fellow Citizens taken Captive on the high Seas to bear Arms against their Country, to become the executioners of their friends and Brethren, or to fall themselves by their Hands.

"He has excited domestic insurrections amongst us and has endeavored to bring on the inhabitants of our frontiers, the merciless Indian Savages, whose known rule of warfare, is an undistinguished destruction of all ages, sexes and conditions.

"In every stage of these Oppressions, We have Petitioned for Redress in the most humble terms: Our repeated Petitions have been answered only by repeated injury. A Prince whose character is thus marked by every act which may define a Tyrant, is unfit to be the ruler of a free people.

"Nor have We been wanting in attentions to our British brethren. We have warned them from time to time of attempts by their legislature to extend an unwarrantable jurisdiction over us. We have reminded them of the circumstances of our emigration and settlement here. We have appealed to their native justice and magnanimity, and we have conjured them by the

CHAPTER 4

ties of our common kindred to disavow these usurpations, which, would inevitably interrupt our connections and correspondence. They too have been deaf to the voice of justice and of consanguinity. We must, therefore, acquiesce in the necessity, which denounces our Separation, and hold them, as we hold the rest of mankind, Enemies in War, in Peace Friends.

"We, therefore, the Representatives of the united States of America, in General Congress, Assembled, appealing to the Supreme Judge of the world for the rectitude of our intentions, do, in the Name, and by Authority of the good People of these Colonies, solemnly publish and declare, That these United Colonies are, and of Right ought to be Free and Independent States; that they are Absolved from all Allegiance to the British Crown, and that all political connection between them and the State of Great Britain, is and ought to be totally dissolved; and that as Free and Independent States, they have full Power to levy War, conclude Peace, contract Alliances, establish Commerce, and to do all other Acts and Things which Independent States may of right do. And for the support of this Declaration, with a firm reliance on the protection of divine Providence, we mutually pledge to each other our Lives, our Fortunes and our sacred Honor."

After reading this document, is it more clear to you now why I said God sent Malcolm X and Martin Luther King Jr. at the same time purposely? If not just keep reading. As you should see, the strategy Malcom X used as a basis for Civil Rights was established by the founding fathers in the Declaration of Independence. The founding fathers, when they were being oppressed and in bondage, stated that because all men were created equal the British did not have the God-given right to usurp authority over them. Because they as a people were being treated unjustly with no visible justice in sight. And the very government that established the rules for their lives were their oppressors, they had a God-given right to rise up.

Now, I'm not saying that it's necessary to rise up against our government. What I am saying is our government should remember the promise it made to God, because God remembers!

Let's next take a peek at the United States Constitution.

The Constitution of the United States

> "**We the People** of the United States, in Order to form a more perfect Union (the action or fact of joining or being joined, especially in a political context), establish (set up on a firm or permanent basis) Justice (just behavior or treatment), insure domestic (existing or occurring inside a particular country; not foreign or international) Tranquility (A peaceful, calm state, without noise, violence, worry, etc.), provide for the common (shared by, coming from, or done by more than one) defense (the action of defending from or resisting attack), promote (support the progress of something , especially a cause, venture, or aim; support or actively encourage) the general (affecting or concerning all or most people, places, or things; widespread) Welfare (the health, happiness, and fortunes of a person or group), and secure the Blessings (empowerment to prosper) of Liberty (the state of being free within society from oppressive restriction imposed by authority on one's way of life, behavior, or political views) to ourselves and our Posterity (all future generations), do ordain (order or decree officially) and establish (set up on a firm or permanent basis) this

Constitution (a body of fundamental principles or established precedents according to which a state or other organization is acknowledged to be governed) for the United States of America."

Now, the Thirteenth Amendment to the United States Constitution abolished slavery and involuntary servitude, except as punishment for a crime. The amendment was passed by the Senate on April 8, 1864, by the House of Representatives on January 31, 1865, and ratified by the required 27 of the then 36 states on December 6, 1865, and proclaimed on December 18. It was the first of the three Reconstruction Amendments adopted following the Civil War.

The Reconstruction Amendments and Subsequent Law

President Abraham Lincoln's Emancipation Proclamation, effective on January 1, 1863, declared that the enslaved in Confederate controlled areas were free. When they escaped to Union lines or federal forces (including now former slaves) advanced south, emancipation occurred without any compensation to the former owners. Texas was the last Confederate territory reached by the Union army.

On June 19, 1865, "Juneteenth," U.S. Army general Gordon Granger arrived in Galveston, Texas, to proclaim the war had ended and so had slavery (in the Confederate states). In the slave owning areas controlled by Union forces on January 1, 1863, state action was used to abolish slavery. The exceptions were New Jersey, Kentucky, and Delaware, where all forms of forced labor were finally ended by the Thirteenth Amendment in December 1865.

In contrast to the other Reconstruction Amendments, the Thirteenth Amendment has rarely been cited in case law, but it has been used to strike down peonage and some race-based discrimination as "badges and incidents of slavery." The Thirteenth Amendment has also been invoked to empower Congress to make laws against modern forms of slavery, such as sex trafficking.

Since 1776, the Union had been divided into states that allowed slavery and states that prohibited it. Slavery was implicitly recognized in the original Constitution in provisions such as Article I, Section 2, Clause 3, commonly known as the Three-Fifths Compromise, which provided that three fifths of each state's enslaved population ("other persons") was to be added to its free population for the purposes of apportioning seats in the United States House of Representatives, its number of Electoral votes, and direct taxes among the states. Article IV, Section 2, provided that slaves held under the laws of one state, who escaped to another state, did not become free, but remained slaves.

Though three million Confederate slaves were in fact eventually freed as a result of Lincoln's Emancipation Proclamation, their postwar status was uncertain. To ensure that abolition was beyond legal challenge, an amendment to the Constitution to that effect was initiated. On April 8, 1864, the Senate passed an amendment to abolish slavery. After one unsuccessful vote and extensive legislative maneuvering by the Lincoln administration, the House followed suit on January 31, 1865. The measure was swiftly ratified by nearly all Northern states, along with a sufficient number of border states (slave states not part of the Confederacy) up to the assassination of President Lincoln.

However, the approval came via his successor, President Andrew Johnson, who encouraged the "reconstructed" Southern states of Alabama, North Carolina, and Georgia to agree, which brought the count to 27 states, leading to its adoption before the end of 1865. Though the Amendment abolished slavery throughout the United States, some African Americans, particularly in the South, were subjected to other forms of involuntary labor, such as under the Black Codes, European-American supremacist violence, and selective enforcement of statutes, as well as other disabilities.

The Black Codes

The Black Codes, sometimes called the Black Laws, were laws which governed the conduct of African Americans (free and freed African Americans). In 1832, James Kent wrote that "in most of the United States, there is a distinction in respect to political privileges, between free European American persons and free African American persons; and in no part of the country do the latter, in point of fact, participate equally with the European Americans, in the exercise of civil and political rights." Although Black Codes existed before the Civil War and many Northern states had them, it was the Southern U.S. states that codified such laws into everyday practice. The best known of them were passed in 1865 and 1866 by Southern states, after the American Civil War, in order to restrict African Americans' freedom, and to compel them to work for low or no wages.

Since the colonial period, colonies and states had passed laws that discriminated against free African Americans. In the South, these were generally included in "slave codes;" the goal was to suppress the influence of free African Americans (particularly after slave rebellions) because of their potential influence on slaves. Restrictions included prohibiting them from voting (North Carolina had allowed this before 1831), bearing arms, gathering in groups for worship, and learning to read and write. The purpose of these laws was to preserve slavery in slave societies.

Before the war, Northern states that had prohibited slavery also enacted laws similar to the slave codes and the later Black Codes. Connecticut, Ohio, Illinois, Indiana, Michigan, and New York enacted laws to discourage free African Americans from residing in those states. They were denied equal political rights, including the right to vote, the right to attend public schools, and the right to equal treatment under the law. Some of the Northern states repealed such laws, those which had them, around the same time that the Civil War ended, and slavery was abolished by constitutional amendment.

In the first two years after the Civil War, European American-dominated Southern legislatures passed Black Codes modeled after the earlier slave codes. Black Codes were part of a larger pattern of European Americans trying to maintain political dominance and suppress the freedmen (a formerly enslaved person who has been released from slavery, usually by manumission, emancipation, or self-purchase), those newly emancipated African Americans. They were particularly concerned with controlling the movement and labor of freedmen, as slavery had been replaced by a free labor system.

Although freedmen had been emancipated, their lives were greatly restricted by the Black Codes. The defining feature of the Black Codes was broad vagrancy law, which allowed local authorities to arrest freed African

Americans for minor infractions and commit them to involuntary labor. This period was the start of the convict lease system, also described as "slavery by another name" by Douglas Blackmon in his 2008 book of this title.

The Thirteenth Amendment and other laws.

Slavery existed and was legal in the United States of America upon its founding in 1776. It was established by European colonization in all of the original thirteen American colonies of British America. Prior to the Thirteenth Amendment, the United States Constitution did not expressly use the words slave or slavery but included several provisions about unfree persons.

The Three-Fifths Compromise, Article I, Section 2, Clause 3 of the Constitution, allocated Congressional representation based "on the whole Number of free Persons" and "three fifths of all other Persons." This clause was a compromise between Southern politicians who wished for enslaved African Americans to be counted as "persons" for congressional representation and Northern politicians rejecting these out of concern of too much power for the South, because representation in the new Congress would be based on population in contrast to the one vote for one state principle in the earlier Continental Congress.

Under the Fugitive Slave Clause, Article IV, Section 2, Clause 3, "No person held to Service or Labor in one State" would be freed by escaping to another. Article I, Section 9, Clause 1 allowed Congress to pass legislation outlawing the "Importation of Persons," which would not be passed until 1808. However, for purposes of the Fifth Amendment, which states that "No person shall be deprived of life, liberty, or property, without due process of law," slaves were understood as property. Although abolitionists used the Fifth Amendment to argue against slavery, it became part of the legal basis in *Dred Scott v. Sandford* (1857) for treating slaves as property.

Stimulated by the philosophy of the Declaration of Independence, between 1777 and 1804, every Northern state provided for the immediate or gradual abolition of slavery. Most of the slaves who were emancipated by such legislation were household servants. No Southern state did so, and the enslaved population of the South continued to grow, peaking at almost four million in 1861.

An abolitionist movement headed by such figures as William Lloyd Garrison grew in strength in the North, calling for the end of slavery nationwide, exacerbating tensions between North and South. The American Colonization Society, an alliance between abolitionists who felt the races should be kept separated and slaveholders who feared the presence of freed African Americans would encourage slave rebellions, called for the emigration of both free African Americans and slaves to Africa, where they would establish independent colonies. Its views were endorsed by politicians such as Henry Clay, who feared that the American abolitionist movement would provoke a civil war. Proposals to eliminate slavery by constitutional amendment were introduced by Representative Arthur Livermore in 1818 and by John Quincy Adams in 1839, but failed to gain significant traction.

As the country continued to expand, the issue of slavery in its new territories became the dominant national issue. The Southern position was that slaves were property and therefore could be moved to the territories like all other forms of property. The 1820 Missouri Compromise provided for the admission of Missouri

CHAPTER 4

as a slave state and Maine as a free state, preserving the Senate's equality between the regions.

In 1846, the Wilmot Proviso was appended to a war appropriations bill to ban slavery in all territories acquired in the Mexican-American War; the Proviso repeatedly passed the House, but not the Senate. The Compromise of 1850 temporarily defused the issue by admitting California as a free state, instituting a stronger Fugitive Slave Act, banning the slave trade in Washington, D.C., and allowing New Mexico and Utah self-determination on the slavery issue.

Despite the compromise, tensions between North and South continued to rise over the subsequent decade, inflamed by, amongst other things, the publication of the 1852 anti-slavery novel *Uncle Tom's Cabin*; fighting between pro-slavery and abolitionist forces in Kansas, beginning in 1854; the 1857 *Dred Scott* decision, which struck down provisions of the Compromise of 1850; abolitionist John Brown's 1859 attempt to start a slave revolt at Harpers Ferry; and the 1860 election of slavery critic Abraham Lincoln to the presidency. The Southern states seceded from the Union in the months following Lincoln's election, forming the Confederate States of America, and beginning the Civil War.

Acting under presidential war powers, Lincoln issued the Emancipation Proclamation on September 22, 1862, with effect on January 1, 1863, which proclaimed the freedom of slaves in the ten states that were still in rebellion. In his State of the Union message to Congress on December 1, 1862, Lincoln also presented a plan for "gradual emancipation and deportation" of slaves.

This plan envisioned three amendments to the Constitution. The first would have required the states to abolish slavery by January 1, 1900. Lincoln's Emancipation Proclamation then proceeded immediately freeing slaves in January 1863 but this did not affect the status of slaves in the border states that had remained loyal to the Union. By December 1863, Lincoln again used his war powers and issued a "Proclamation for Amnesty and Reconstruction," which offered Southern states a chance to peacefully rejoin the Union if they immediately abolished slavery and collected loyalty oaths from 10% of their voting population.

Southern states did not readily accept the deal, and the status of slavery remained uncertain. In the final years of the Civil War, Union lawmakers debated various proposals for Reconstruction. Some of these called for a constitutional amendment to abolish slavery nationally and permanently. On December 14, 1863, a bill proposing such an amendment was introduced by Representative James Mitchell Ashley of Ohio. Representative James F. Wilson of Iowa soon followed with a similar proposal. On January 11, 1864, Senator John B. Henderson of Missouri submitted a joint resolution for a constitutional amendment abolishing slavery. The Senate Judiciary Committee, chaired by Lyman Trumbull of Illinois, became involved in merging different proposals for an amendment.

Radical Republicans led by Massachusetts Senator Charles Sumner and Pennsylvania Representative Thaddeus Stevens sought a more expansive version of the amendment. On February 8, 1864, Sumner submitted a constitutional amendment stating: "All persons are equal before the law, so that no person can hold another as a slave; and the Congress shall have power to make all laws necessary and proper to carry this declaration into effect everywhere in the United States."

Sumner tried to have his amendment sent to his committee, rather than the Trumbull controlled Judiciary Committee, but the Senate refused. On February 10, the Senate Judiciary Committee presented the Senate with an amendment proposal based on drafts of Ashley, Wilson, and Henderson. The Committee's version used text from the Northwest Ordinance of 1787, which stipulates, "There shall be neither slavery nor involuntary servitude in the said territory, otherwise than in the punishment of crimes whereof the party shall have been duly convicted."

Though using Henderson's proposed amendment as the basis for its new draft, the Judiciary Committee removed language that would have allowed a constitutional amendment to be adopted with only a majority vote in each House of Congress and ratification by two thirds of the states (instead of two thirds and three fourths, respectively).

The Senate passed the amendment on April 8, 1864, by a vote of 38 to 6; 2 Democrats, Reverdy Johnson of Maryland and James Nesmith of Oregon, voted for the amendment. However, just over two months later on June 15, the House failed to do so, with 93 in favor and 65 against, 13 votes short of the two thirds vote needed for passage. The vote split largely along party lines, with Republicans supporting and Democrats opposing.

In the 1864 presidential race, former Free Soil Party candidate John C. Frémont threatened a third party run opposing Lincoln, this time on a platform endorsing an anti-slavery amendment. The Republican Party platform had, as yet failed to include a similar plank, though Lincoln endorsed the amendment in a letter accepting his nomination. Frémont withdrew from the race on September 22, 1864 and endorsed Lincoln.

With no Southern states represented, few members of Congress pushed moral and religious arguments in favor of slavery. Democrats who opposed the amendment generally made arguments based on federalism and states' rights. Some argued that the proposed change so violated the spirit of the Constitution it would not be a valid "amendment" but would instead constitute "revolution." Representative White, among other opponents, warned that the amendment would lead to full citizenship for African Americans.

Republicans portrayed slavery as uncivilized and argued for abolition as a necessary step in national progress. Amendment supporters also argued that the slave system had negative effects on European American people. These included the lower wages resulting from competition with forced labor, as well as repression of abolitionist European Americans in the South. Advocates said ending slavery would restore the First Amendment and other constitutional rights violated by censorship and intimidation in slave states.

European Americans, Northern Republicans, and some Democrats became excited about an abolition amendment, therefore holding meetings and issuing resolutions. Many African Americans though, particularly in the South, focused more on land ownership and education as the key to liberation. As slavery began to seem politically untenable, an array of Northern Democrats successively announced their support for the amendment, including Representative James Brooks, Senator Reverdy Johnson, and the powerful New York political machine known as Tammany Hall.

CHAPTER 4

President Lincoln had concerns that the Emancipation Proclamation of 1863 might be reversed or found invalid by the judiciary after the war. He saw constitutional amendment as a more permanent solution. He had remained outwardly neutral on the amendment because he considered it politically too dangerous. Nonetheless, Lincoln's 1864 election platform resolved to abolish slavery by constitutional amendment.

After winning reelection in the election of 1864, Lincoln made the passage of the Thirteenth Amendment his top legislative priority. He began with his efforts in Congress during its "lame duck" session, in which many members of Congress had already seen their successors elected; most would be concerned about unemployment and lack of income, and none needed to fear the electoral consequences of cooperation. Popular support for the amendment mounted and Lincoln urged Congress on in his December 6, 1864 State of the Union Address: "there is only a question of time as to when the proposed amendment will go to the States for their action. And as it is to so go at all events, may we not agree that the sooner the better?"

Lincoln instructed Secretary of State William H. Seward, Representative John B. Alley, and others to procure votes by any means necessary, and they promised government posts and campaign contributions to outgoing Democrats willing to switch sides. Seward had a large fund for direct bribes. Ashley, who reintroduced the measure into the House, also lobbied several Democrats to vote in favor of the measure. Representative Thaddeus Stevens later commented that "the greatest measure of the nineteenth century was passed by corruption aided and abetted by the purest man in America." However,

Lincoln's precise role in making deals for votes remains unknown.

Republicans in Congress claimed a mandate for abolition, having gained in the elections for Senate and House. The 1864 Democratic vice-presidential nominee, Representative George H. Pendleton, led opposition to the measure. Republicans toned down their language of radical equality in order to broaden the amendment's coalition of supporters. In order to reassure critics worried that the amendment would tear apart the social fabric, some Republicans explicitly promised the amendment would leave patriarchy intact.

In mid-January 1865, Speaker of the House Schuyler Colfax estimated the amendment to be five votes short of passage. Ashley postponed the vote. At this point, Lincoln intensified his push for the amendment, making direct emotional appeals to particular members of Congress. On January 31, 1865, the House called another vote on the amendment, with neither side being certain of the outcome. With a total of 183 House members (one seat was vacant after Reuben Fenton was elected governor), 122 would have to vote "aye" to secure passage of the resolution; however, 8 Democrats abstained, reducing the number to 117.

Every Republican (84), Independent Republican (2), and Unconditional Unionist (16) supported the measure, as well as 14 Democrats, almost all of them lame ducks, and 3 Unionists. The amendment finally passed by a vote of 119 to 56, narrowly reaching the required two thirds majority. The House exploded into celebration, with some members openly weeping. African American onlookers, who had only been allowed to attend Congressional sessions since the previous year, cheered from the galleries.

While the Constitution does not provide the President any formal role in the amendment process, the joint resolution was sent to Lincoln for his signature. Under the usual signatures of the Speaker of the House and the President of the Senate, President Lincoln wrote the word "Approved" and added his signature to the joint resolution on February 1, 1865. On February 7, Congress passed a resolution affirming that the Presidential signature was unnecessary. The Thirteenth Amendment is the only ratified amendment signed by a President, although James Buchanan had signed the Corwin Amendment that the 36th Congress had adopted and sent to the states in March 1861.

Ratification.

On February 1, 1865, when the proposed amendment was submitted to the states for ratification, there were 36 states in the U.S., including those that had been in rebellion. At least 27 states had to ratify the amendment for it to come into force. By the end of February, 18 states had ratified the amendment. Among them were the ex-Confederate states of Virginia and Louisiana, where ratifications were submitted by Reconstruction governments. These, along with subsequent ratifications from Arkansas and Tennessee, raised the issues of how many seceded states had legally valid legislatures and if there were fewer legislatures than states, whether Article V required ratification by three fourths of the states or three fourths of the legally valid state legislatures.

President Lincoln, in his last speech, on April 11, 1865, called the question about whether the Southern states were in or out of the Union a "pernicious abstraction." He declared they were not "in their proper practical relation with the Union;" whence everyone's object should be to restore that relation. ^{Lincoln was assassinated} three days later.

With Congress out of session, the new President, Andrew Johnson, began a period known as "Presidential Reconstruction," in which he personally oversaw the creation of new state governments throughout the South. He oversaw the convening of state political conventions populated by delegates whom he deemed to be loyal. Three leading issues came before the conventions: Secession itself, the abolition of slavery, and the Confederate war debt.

Alabama, Florida, Georgia, Mississippi, North Carolina, and South Carolina held conventions in 1865, while Texas' convention did not organize until March 1866. Johnson hoped to prevent deliberation over whether to readmit the Southern states by accomplishing full ratification before Congress reconvened in December. He believed he could silence those who wished to deny the Southern states their place in the Union by pointing to how essential their assent had been to the successful ratification of the Thirteenth Amendment.

Direct negotiations between state governments and the Johnson administration ensued. As the summer wore on, administration officials began giving assurances of the measure's limited scope with their demands for ratification. Johnson himself suggested directly to the governors of Mississippi and North Carolina that they could proactively control the allocation of rights to freedmen. Though Johnson obviously expected the freed people to enjoy at least some civil rights, including, as he specified, the right to testify in court, he wanted state lawmakers to know that the power to confer such rights would remain with the states.

When South Carolina provisional governor Benjamin Franklin Perry objected to the scope of the amendment's enforcement clause, Secretary of State Seward responded by telegraph that in fact the second clause "is really restraining in its effect, instead of enlarging the powers of Congress." Politicians throughout the South were concerned that Congress might cite the amendment's enforcement powers as a way to authorize black suffrage (African American's right to vote).

When South Carolina ratified the Amendment in November 1865, it issued its own interpretive declaration that "any attempt by Congress toward legislating upon the political status of former slaves, or their civil relations, would be contrary to the Constitution of the United States." Alabama and Louisiana also declared that their ratification did not imply federal power to legislate on the status of former slaves. During the first week of December, North Carolina and Georgia gave the amendment the final votes needed for it to become part of the Constitution.

The first 27 states to ratify the Amendment were:
1. Illinois: February 1, 1865
2. Rhode Island: February 2, 1865
3. Michigan: February 3, 1865
4. Maryland: February 3, 1865
5. New York: February 3, 1865
6. Pennsylvania: February 3, 1865
7. West Virginia: February 3, 1865
8. Missouri: February 6, 1865
9. Maine: February 7, 1865
10. Kansas: February 7, 1865

THE DECLARATION OF INDEPENDENCE

11. Massachusetts: February 7, 1865
12. Virginia: February 9, 1865
13. Ohio: February 10, 1865
14. Indiana: February 13, 1865
15. Nevada: February 16, 1865
16. Louisiana: February 17, 1865
17. Minnesota: February 23, 1865
18. Wisconsin: February 24, 1865
19. Vermont: March 9, 1865
20. Tennessee: April 7, 1865
21. Arkansas: April 14, 1865
22. Connecticut: May 4, 1865
23. New Hampshire: July 1, 1865
24. South Carolina: November 13, 1865
25. Alabama: December 2, 1865
26. North Carolina: December 4, 1865
27. Georgia: December 6, 1865

Having been ratified by the legislatures of three fourths of the states (27 of the 36 states, including those that had been in rebellion), Secretary of State Seward, on December 18, 1865, certified that the Thirteenth Amendment had become valid, to all intents and purposes, as a part of the Constitution. Included on the enrolled list of ratifying states were the three ex-Confederate states that had given their assent, but with strings attached. Seward accepted their affirmative votes and brushed aside their interpretive declarations without comment, challenge, or acknowledgment.

The Thirteenth Amendment was subsequently ratified by the other states, as follows:

28. Oregon: December 8, 1865
29. California: December 19, 1865

30. Florida: December 28, 1865 (reaffirmed June 9, 1868)
31. Iowa: January 15, 1866
32. New Jersey: January 23, 1866 (after rejection March 16, 1865)
33. Texas: February 18, 1870
34. Delaware: February 12, 1901 (after rejection February 8, 1865)
35. Kentucky: March 18, 1976 (after rejection February 24, 1865)
36. Mississippi: March 16, 1995; certified February 7, 2013 (after rejection December 5, 1865)

Abolition

The immediate impact of the amendment was to make the entire pre-war system of chattel slavery in the U.S. illegal. The impact of the abolition of slavery was felt quickly. When the Thirteenth Amendment became operational, the scope of Lincoln's 1863 Emancipation Proclamation was widened to include the entire nation. Although the majority of Kentucky's slaves had been emancipated, 65,000–100,000 people remained to be legally freed when the amendment went into effect on December 18. In Delaware, where a large number of slaves had escaped during the war, nine hundred people became legally free. With slavery abolished, the Fugitive Slave Clause remained in place but became largely moot.

Despite being rendered unconstitutional, slavery continued in areas under the jurisdiction of Native American tribes beyond ratification. The federal government negotiated new treaties with the "Five Civilized Tribes" (the word civilized was applied to the five tribes because, broadly speaking, they had developed extensive economic ties with European Americans or had assimilated into American settler culture). Some members of these Southeastern Tribes had adopted European clothing, spoke English, practice Christianity, and even owned slaves. The five tribes included the (1) Cherokee, (2) Creek, (3) Choctaw, (4) Chickasaw, and (5) Seminole. In 1866, they agreed to end slavery.

The Three-Fifths Compromise in the original Constitution counted, for purposes of allocating taxes and seats in the House of Representatives, all "free persons," and three fifths of "other persons" (slaves) but excluded untaxed Native Americans. The freeing of all slaves made the Three-Fifths clause moot. Compared to the pre-war system, it also had the effect of increasing the political power of former slave-holding states by increasing their share of seats in the House of Representatives, and consequently their share in the Electoral College (where the number of a state's electoral votes, under Article II of the United States Constitution, is tied to the size of its congressional delegation).

Even as the Thirteenth Amendment was working its way through the ratification process, Republicans in Congress grew increasingly concerned about the potential for there to be a large increase in the congressional representation of the Democratic dominated Southern states. Because the full population of freed slaves would be counted rather than three fifths, the Southern states would dramatically increase their power in the population-based House of Representatives. Republicans hoped to offset this advantage by attracting and protecting votes of the newly enfranchised African American population. They would eventually attempt to address this issue in section 2 of the Fourteenth Amendment.

CHAPTER 4

Slavery in Another Guise

Southern culture remained deeply racist, and those African Americans who remained in the South faced a dangerous situation. J. J. Gries reported to the Joint Committee on Reconstruction: "There is a kind of innate feeling, a lingering hope among many in the South that slavery will be regalvanized in some shape or other. They tried by their laws to make a worse slavery than there was before, for the freedman has not the protection which the master from interest gave him before."

W. E. B. Du Bois wrote in 1935:

> "Slavery was not abolished even after the Thirteenth Amendment. There were four million freedmen and most of them on the same plantation, doing the same work they did before emancipation, except as their work had been interrupted and changed by the upheaval of war. Moreover, they were getting about the same wages and apparently were going to be subject to slave codes modified only in name. There were among them thousands of fugitives in the camps of the soldiers or on the streets of the cities, homeless, sick, and impoverished. They had been freed practically with no land nor money, and save in exceptional cases, without legal status, and without protection."

Official emancipation did not substantially alter the economic situation of most African Americans who remained in the south.

As the amendment still permitted labor as punishment for convicted criminals, Southern states responded with what historian Douglas A. Blackmon called "an array of interlocking laws essentially intended to criminalize African American life." These laws, passed or updated after emancipation, were known as Black Codes. Mississippi was the first state to pass such codes, with an 1865 law titled "An Act to confer Civil Rights on Freedmen." The Mississippi law required African American workers to contract with European American farmers by January 1 of each year or face punishment for vagrancy.

African Americans could be sentenced to forced labor for crimes including petty theft, using obscene language, or selling cotton after sunset. States passed new, strict vagrancy laws that were selectively enforced against African Americans without European American protectors. The labor of these convicts was then sold to farms, factories, lumber camps, quarries, and mines.

After its ratification of the Thirteenth Amendment in November 1865, the South Carolina legislature immediately began to legislate Black Codes. The Black Codes created a separate set of laws, punishments, and acceptable behaviors for anyone with more than one African American great-grandparent. Under these Codes, African Americans could only work as farmers or servants and had few Constitutional rights. Restrictions on African American land ownership threatened to make economic subservience permanent. Some states mandated indefinitely long periods of child "apprenticeship." Some laws did not target African Americans specifically, but instead affected farm workers, most of whom were African American. At the same time, many states passed laws to actively prevent African Americans from acquiring property.

As its first enforcement legislation, Congress passed the Civil Rights Act of 1866, guaranteeing African Americans citizenship and equal protection of the law, though not the right to vote. The amendment was also used as authorizing several Freedmen's Bureau bills. President Andrew Johnson vetoed these bills, but Congress overrode his vetoes to pass the Civil Rights Act and the Second Freedmen's Bureau Bill. Proponents of the Act, including Trumbull and Wilson, argued that Section 2 of the Thirteenth Amendment authorized the federal government to legislate civil rights for the States. Others disagreed, maintaining that inequality conditions were distinct from slavery.

Seeking more substantial justification, and fearing that future opponents would again seek to overturn the legislation, Congress and the states added additional protections to the Constitution: The Fourteenth Amendment (1868) defining citizenship and mandating equal protection under the law, and the Fifteenth Amendment (1870) banning racial voting restrictions. The Freedmen's Bureau enforced the amendment locally, providing a degree of support for people subject to the Black Codes. Reciprocally, the Thirteenth Amendment established the Bureau's legal basis to operate in Kentucky. The Civil Rights Act circumvented racism in local jurisdictions by allowing African Americans access to the federal courts. The Enforcement Acts of 1870–1871 and the Civil Rights Act of 1875, in combating the violence and intimidation of European American supremacy, were also part of the effort to end slave conditions for Southern African Americans. However, the effect of these laws waned as political will diminished and the federal government lost authority in the South, particularly after the Compromise of 1877 ended Reconstruction in exchange for a Republican presidency.

Peonage

Southern business owners sought to reproduce the profitable arrangement of slavery with a system called peonage (also called debt slavery or debt servitude, this was a system where an employer compelled a worker to pay off a debt with work), in which disproportionately African American workers were entrapped by loans and compelled to work indefinitely due to the resulting debt. Peonage continued well through Reconstruction and ensnared a large proportion of African American workers in the South.

These workers remained destitute and persecuted, forced to work dangerous jobs and further confined legally by the racist Jim Crow laws that governed the South. Peonage differed from chattel slavery because it was not strictly hereditary and did not allow the sale of people in exactly the same fashion. However, a person's debt and by extension a person could still be sold, and the system resembled antebellum slavery in many ways.

Slavery in New Mexico also continued *de facto* in the form of peonage, which became a Spanish colonial tradition so to work around the prohibition of hereditary slavery by the New Laws of 1542. Though this practice was rendered unconstitutional by the Thirteenth Amendment, enforcement was lax. The Peonage Act of 1867 specifically mentioned New Mexico and increased enforcement by banning nationwide "the holding of any person to service or labor under the system known as peonage," specifically banning "the voluntary or involuntary service or labor of any persons as peons (day laborer or unskilled farm worker, attendant, orderly, or assistant, etc.) in liquidation of any debt or obligation, or otherwise."

In 1939, the Department of Justice created the Civil Rights Section, which focused primarily on First Amendment and labor rights. The increasing scrutiny of totalitarianism in the lead up to World War II brought increased attention to issues of slavery and involuntary servitude, abroad and at home. The U.S. sought to counter foreign propaganda and increase its credibility on the race issue by combatting the Southern peonage system. Under the leadership of Attorney General Francis Biddle, the Civil Rights Section invoked the constitutional amendments and legislation of the Reconstruction Era as the basis for its actions.

In 1947, the DOJ successfully prosecuted Elizabeth Ingalls for keeping domestic servant Dora L. Jones in conditions of slavery. The court found that Jones "was a person wholly subject to the will of defendant; that she was one who had no freedom of action and whose person and services were wholly under the control of defendant and who was in a state of enforced compulsory service to the defendant."

The Thirteenth Amendment enjoyed a swell of attention during this period, between *Brown v. Board of Education* (1954) until *Jones v. Alfred H. Mayer Co.* (1968), but it was eclipsed by the Fourteenth Amendment.

Penal Labor

The Thirteenth Amendment exempts penal labor from its prohibition of forced labor. This allows prisoners who have been convicted of crimes (not those merely awaiting trial) to be required to perform labor or else face punishment while in custody.

Few records of the committee's deliberations during the drafting of the Thirteenth Amendment survive, and the debate that followed both in Congress and in the state legislatures featured almost no discussion of this provision. It was apparently considered noncontroversial at the time, or at least legislators gave it little thought. The drafters based the amendment's phrasing on the Northwest Ordinance of 1787, which features an identical exception for prisoners. Thomas Jefferson authored an early version of that ordinance's anti-slavery clause, including the exception of punishment for a crime, and also sought to prohibit slavery in general after 1800. Jefferson was an admirer of the works of Italian criminologist Cesare Beccaria. Beccaria's *On Crimes and Punishments* suggested that the death penalty should be abolished and replaced with a lifetime of enslavement for the worst criminals.

Various commentators have accused states of abusing this provision to reestablish systems similar to slavery, or of otherwise exploiting such labor in a manner unfair to local labor. The Black Codes in the South criminalized "vagrancy," which was largely enforced against freed slaves. Later, convict lease programs in the South allowed local plantations to rent inexpensive prisoner labor. While many of these programs have been phased out (leasing of convicts was forbidden by President Franklin Roosevelt in 1941), prison labor continues in the U.S. under a variety of justifications.

Prison labor programs vary widely; some are uncompensated prison maintenance tasks, some are for local government maintenance tasks, some are for local businesses, and others are closer to internships. Modern rationales for prison labor programs often include reduction of recidivism and re-acclimation to society. The idea is that such labor programs will make it easier for the prisoner upon release to find gainful employment rather than relapse to criminality. However, this topic is not well studied, and much of the work offered is so menial as to be unlikely to improve employment prospects. As of 2022, most prison labor programs do compensate prisoners, but generally with very low wages. What wages they do earn are often heavily garnished, with as much as 80% of a prisoner's paycheck withheld in the harshest cases.

In 2018, artist and entertainer Kanye West advocated for repealing the Thirteenth Amendment's exception for penal labor in a meeting with Former President Donald Trump, calling the exception a "trap door." In late 2020, Senator Jeff Merkley (D-OR) and Representative William Lacy Clay (D-MO) introduced a resolution to create a new amendment to close this loophole.

Kanye West seems to have been referring to the amendment's "exception clause," the part that allows slavery and involuntary servitude to continue as a punishment for crime whereof the party shall have been duly convicted.

When Congress debated the amendment, anti-slavery Republican Senator Charles Sumner of Massachusetts spoke out forcefully against allowing slavery to continue in the penal system, urging the Senate Judiciary Committee to remove that language. During floor debates in 1864, Sumner noted that the exact language of the 13th Amendment can be traced to the Northwest Ordinance of 1787, which outlawed slavery in the Northwest Territory, except as a punishment for a crime, at a time when there were no prisons. "Why adopt last century's code of human decency," he asked. He said that in 1787 "it was the habit in certain parts of the country to doom people as slaves for life as a punishment for crime" but in this context, the words "do no good."

Sumner got his told-you-so moment in the years after the amendment's passage, when states started using the 13th Amendment to re-enslave people convicted of crimes for a term of years, selling them at auction to the highest bidder. In the Southern states, "tens of thousands of people, overwhelmingly black, were leased by the state to plantation owners, privately owned railroad yards, coal mines and road-building chain gangs and made to work under the whip from dusk till dawn, often as punishment for petty crimes such as vagrancy or theft." The Oscar-nominated documentary 13th analyzed the connection between the amendment and the prison-industrial complex. "The 13th Amendment's exception clause allowed the convict-leasing system to flourish and grow, and it became the dominant form of imprisonment throughout the South. It served as a blueprint for the harsh, retributionist imprisonment that became, tragically, the dominant form of American incarceration."

Every day, more than 800,000 prisoners are put to work, doing cleaning, cooking, and lawn mowing. In some states, they are forced to work, and the pay can be as low as 4 cents an hour. The exception clause in the 13th Amendment has been used to defend these practices.

Case Law and the Thirteenth Amendment
In contrast to the other "Reconstruction Amendments," the Thirteenth Amendment was rarely cited in later case law. As historian Amy Dru Stanley summarizes, "beyond a handful of landmark rulings striking down debt peonage, flagrant involuntary servitude, and some

instances of race-based violence and discrimination, the Thirteenth Amendment has never been a potent source of rights claims."

United States v. Rhodes (1866), one of the first Thirteenth Amendment cases, tested the constitutionality of provisions in the Civil Rights Act of 1866 that granted African Americans redress in the federal courts. Kentucky law prohibited African Americans from testifying against European Americans, an arrangement which compromised the ability of Nancy Talbot ("a citizen of the United States of the African race") to reach justice against a European American person accused of robbing her. After Talbot attempted to try the case in federal court, the Kentucky Supreme Court ruled this federal option unconstitutional. Noah Swayne (a Supreme Court justice sitting on the Kentucky Circuit Court) overturned the Kentucky decision, holding that without the material enforcement provided by the Civil Rights Act, slavery would not truly be abolished. With *In Re Turner* (1867), Chief Justice Salmon P. Chase ordered freedom for Elizabeth Turner, a former slave in Maryland who became indentured to her former master.

In *Blyew v. United States*, (1872) the Supreme Court heard another Civil Rights Act case relating to federal courts in Kentucky. John Blyew and George Kennard were European American men visiting the cabin of an African American family, the Fosters. Blyew apparently became angry with sixteen-year-old Richard Foster and hit him twice in the head with an ax. Blyew and Kennard killed Richard's parents, Sallie and Jack Foster, and his blind grandmother, Lucy Armstrong. They severely wounded the Fosters' two young daughters. Kentucky courts would not allow the Foster children to testify against Blyew and Kennard. Federal courts, authorized by the Civil Rights Act, found Blyew and Kennard guilty of murder. The Supreme Court ruled that the Foster children did not have standing in federal courts because only living people could take advantage of the Act. In doing so, the Courts effectively ruled that the Thirteenth Amendment did not permit a federal remedy in murder cases. Swayne and Joseph P. Bradley dissented, maintaining that in order to have meaningful effects, the Thirteenth Amendment would have to address systemic racial oppression.

The *Blyew* case set a precedent in state and federal courts that led to the erosion of Congress›s Thirteenth Amendment powers. The Supreme Court continued along this path in the *Slaughter-House Cases* (1873), which upheld a state sanctioned monopoly of European American butchers. In *United States v. Cruikshank* (1876), the Court ignored Thirteenth Amendment dicta from a circuit court decision to exonerate perpetrators of the Colfax massacre and invalidate the Enforcement Act of 1870.

The Thirteenth Amendment is not solely a ban on chattel slavery; it also covers a much broader array of labor arrangements and social deprivations. As the U.S. Supreme Court explicated in the *Slaughter-House Cases* with respect to the Fourteenth and Fifteenth Amendment, and the Thirteenth Amendment in particular:

"Undoubtedly while African slavery alone was in the mind of the Congress which proposed the thirteenth article, it forbids any other kind of slavery, now or hereafter. If Mexican peonage or the Chinese coolie labor system shall develop slavery of the Mexican or Chinese race within our territory, this amendment may safely be trusted to make it void. And so, if other rights are assailed by the States which properly and necessarily fall within the protection of these articles, that protection will apply, though the party interested may not be of African descent. But what we do say, and what we wish to be understood is, that in any fair and just construction of any section or phrase of these amendments, it is necessary to look to the purpose which we have said was the pervading spirit of them all, the evil which they were designed to remedy, and the process of continued addition to the Constitution, until that purpose was supposed to be accomplished, as far as constitutional law can accomplish it."

In the *Civil Rights Cases* (1883), the Supreme Court reviewed five consolidated cases dealing with the Civil Rights Act of 1875, which outlawed racial discrimination at "inns, public conveyances on land or water, theaters, and other places of public amusement." The Court ruled that the Thirteenth Amendment did not ban most forms of racial discrimination by non-government actors.

In the majority decision, Bradley wrote (again in non-binding dicta) that the Thirteenth Amendment empowered Congress to attack "badges and incidents of slavery." However, he distinguished between "fundamental rights" of citizenship, protected by the Thirteenth Amendment, and the "social rights of men and races in the community." The majority opinion held that "it would be running the slavery argument into the ground to make it apply to every act of discrimination which a person may see fit to make as to guests he will entertain, or as to the people he will take into his coach or cab or car; or admit to his concert or theatre, or deal with in other matters of intercourse or business." In his solitary dissent, John Marshall Harlan (a Kentucky lawyer who changed his mind about civil rights law after witnessing organized racist violence) argued that «such discrimination practiced by corporations and individuals in the exercise of their public or quasi-public functions is a badge of servitude, the imposition of which congress may prevent under its power.»

The Court in the *Civil Rights Cases* also held that appropriate legislation under the amendment could go beyond nullifying state laws establishing or upholding slavery, because the amendment «has a reflex character also, establishing and decreeing universal civil and political freedom throughout the United States" and thus Congress was empowered "to pass all laws necessary and proper for abolishing all badges and incidents of slavery in the United States."

The Court stated about the amendment's scope:

"This amendment, as well as the Fourteenth, is undoubtedly self-executing, without any ancillary legislation, so far as its terms are applicable to any existing state of circumstances. By its own unaided force and effect, it abolished slavery and established universal freedom. Still, legislation may be necessary and proper to meet all the various cases and circumstances to be affected by it, and to prescribe proper modes of redress for its violation in letter or spirit. And such legislation may be primary and direct in its character, for the amendment is not a mere prohibition of State laws establishing or upholding slavery, but an absolute declaration that slavery or involuntary servitude shall not exist in any part of the United States."

Attorneys in *Plessy v. Ferguson* (1896) argued that racial segregation involved «observances of a servile character coincident with the incidents of slavery," in violation of the Thirteenth Amendment. In their brief to the Supreme Court, Plessy's lawyers wrote that "distinction of race and caste" was inherently unconstitutional. The Supreme Court rejected this reasoning and upheld state laws enforcing segregation under the "separate but equal" doctrine.

In the (7–1) majority decision, the Court found that "a statute which implies merely a legal distinction between the European American and African American races, a distinction which is founded on the color of the two races and which must always exist so long as European American men are distinguished from the other race by color, has no tendency to destroy the legal equality of the two races, or reestablish a state of involuntary servitude." Harlan dissented, writing, "The thin disguise of 'equal' accommodations for passengers in railroad coaches will not mislead anyone, nor atone for the wrong this day done."

In *Hodges v. United States* (1906), the Court struck down a federal statute providing for the punishment of two or more people who "conspire to injure, oppress, threaten or intimidate any citizen in the free exercise or enjoyment of any right or privilege secured to him by the Constitution or laws of the United States." A group of European American men in Arkansas conspired to violently prevent eight African American workers from performing their jobs at a lumber mill; the group was convicted by a federal grand jury. The Supreme Court ruled that the federal statute, which outlawed conspiracies to deprive citizens of their liberty, was not authorized by the Thirteenth Amendment. It held that "no mere personal assault or trespass or appropriation operates to reduce the individual to a condition of slavery." Harlan dissented, maintaining his opinion that the Thirteenth

Amendment should protect freedom beyond "physical restraint." *Corrigan v. Buckley* (1922) reaffirmed the interpretation from Hodges, finding that the amendment does not apply to restrictive covenants.

Enforcement of federal civil rights law in the South created numerous peonage cases, which slowly traveled up through the judiciary. The Supreme Court ruled in *Clyatt v. United States* (1905) that peonage was involuntary servitude. It held that although employers sometimes described their workers› entry into contract as voluntary, the servitude of peonage was always (by definition) involuntary.

In *Bailey v. Alabama* the U.S. Supreme Court reaffirmed its holding that the Thirteenth Amendment is not solely a ban on chattel slavery, it also covers a much broader array of labor arrangements and social deprivations. In addition to the aforesaid the Court also ruled on Congress enforcement power under the Thirteenth Amendment. The Court said:

"The plain intention [of the amendment] was to abolish slavery of whatever name and form and all its badges and incidents; to render impossible any state of bondage; to make labor free, by prohibiting that control by which the personal service of one man is disposed of or coerced for another's benefit, which is the essence of involuntary servitude. While the Amendment was self-executing, so far as its terms were applicable to any existing condition, Congress was authorized to secure its complete enforcement by appropriate legislation."

A Turning Point
Legal histories cite *Jones v. Alfred H. Mayer Co.* (1968) as a turning point of Thirteen Amendment jurisprudence.

The Supreme Court confirmed in Jones that Congress may act «rationally» to prevent private actors from imposing «badges and incidents of servitude." The Joneses were an African American couple in St. Louis County, Missouri, who sued a real estate company for refusing to sell them a house.

The Court held that "Congress has the power under the Thirteenth Amendment rationally to determine what are the badges and the incidents of slavery, and the authority to translate that determination into effective legislation. This Court recognized long ago that, whatever else they may have encompassed, the badges and incidents of slavery, its burdens and disabilities, included restraints upon those fundamental rights which are the essence of civil freedom, namely, the same right, to inherit, purchase, lease, sell and convey property, as is enjoyed by European American citizens." Civil Rights Cases, 109 U. S. 3, 109 U. S. 22.

Just as the Black Codes, enacted after the Civil War to restrict the free exercise of those rights, were substitutes for the slave system, so the exclusion of African Americans from European American communities became a substitute for the Black Codes. And when racial discrimination herds men into ghettos and makes their ability to buy property turn on the color of their skin, then it too is a relic of slavery.

African American citizens, North and South, who saw in the Thirteenth Amendment a promise of freedom, freedom to "go and come at pleasure" and to "buy and sell when they please," would be left with "a mere paper guarantee" if Congress were powerless to assure that a dollar in the hands of an African American will purchase the same thing as a dollar in the hands of a European American. At the very least, the freedom that Congress is empowered to secure under the Thirteenth Amendment includes the freedom to buy whatever a European American can buy, the right to live wherever a European American can live. If Congress cannot say that being free means at least this much, then the Thirteenth Amendment made a promise the nation cannot or better yet, is not, willing to keep.

Other Applications of the Thirteenth Amendment

The Court in *Jones* reopened the issue of linking racism in contemporary society to the history of slavery in the United States. The *Jones* precedent has been used to justify Congressional action to protect migrant workers and target sex trafficking. The direct enforcement power found in the Thirteenth Amendment contrasts with that of the Fourteenth, which allows only responses to institutional discrimination of state actors (a person who is acting on behalf of a governmental body).

The Supreme Court has taken an especially narrow view of involuntary servitude claims made by people not descended from African slaves. In *Robertson v. Baldwin* (1897), a group of merchant seamen challenged federal statutes which criminalized a seaman›s failure to complete their contractual term of service. The Court ruled that seamen›s contracts had been considered unique from time immemorial, and that «the amendment was not intended to introduce any novel doctrine with respect to certain descriptions of service which have always been treated as exceptional.» In this case, as in numerous «badges and incidents» cases, Justice Harlan authored a dissent favoring broader Thirteenth Amendment protections.

In *Selective Draft Law Cases*, the Supreme Court ruled that the military draft was not "involuntary servitude." In *United States v. Kozminski*, the Supreme Court ruled that the Thirteenth Amendment did not prohibit compulsion of servitude through psychological coercion. *Kozminski* defined involuntary servitude for purposes of criminal prosecution as «a condition of servitude in which the victim is forced to work for the defendant by the use or threat of physical restraint or physical injury or by the use or threat of coercion through law or the legal process. This definition encompasses cases in which the defendant holds the victim in servitude by placing him or her in fear of such physical restraint or injury or legal coercion.»

The U.S. Courts of Appeals, in *Immediato v. Rye Neck School District*, *Herndon v. Chapel Hill*, and *Steirer v. Bethlehem School District*, have ruled that the use of community service as a high school graduation requirement did not violate the Thirteenth Amendment.

During the six decades following the 1804 ratification of the Twelfth Amendment two proposals to amend the Constitution were adopted by Congress and sent to the states for ratification. Neither has been ratified by the number of states necessary to become part of the Constitution. Each is referred to as Article Thirteen, as was the successful Thirteenth Amendment, in the joint resolution passed by Congress:

(1) The Titles of Nobility Amendment (pending before the states since May 1, 1810) would, if ratified, strip citizenship from any United States citizen who accepts a title of nobility or honor from a foreign country without the consent of Congress.

(2) The Corwin Amendment (pending before the states since March 2, 1861) would, if ratified, shield "domestic institutions" of the states (in 1861 this was a common euphemism for slavery) from the constitutional

amendment process and from abolition or interference by Congress.

Right of Assembly
Martin Luther King Jr faced oppression when it came to The Right of Assembly, as outlined in the First Amendment:

The Right of Assembly is the individual right of people to come together and collectively express, promote, pursue, and defend their collective or shared ideas. This right is equally important as those of free speech and free press, because, as observed by the Supreme Court of the United States in *De Jonge v. Oregon*, 299 U.S. 353, 364, 365 (1937), the right of peaceable assembly is "cognate to those of free speech and free press and is equally fundamental. It is one that cannot be denied without violating those fundamental principles of liberty and justice which lie at the base of all civil and political institutions principles which the Fourteenth Amendment embodies in the general terms of its due process clause. The holding of meetings for peaceable political action cannot be proscribed. Those who assist in the conduct of such meetings cannot be branded as criminals on that score. The question is not as to the auspices under which the meeting is held but as to its purpose; not as to the relations of the speakers, but whether their utterances transcend the bounds of the freedom of speech which the Constitution protects."

The right of peaceable assembly was originally distinguished from the right to petition. In *United States v. Cruikshank* (1875), the first case in which the right to assembly was before the Supreme Court, the court broadly declared the outlines of the right of assembly and its connection to the right of petition:

CHAPTER 4

"The right of the people peaceably to assemble for the purpose of petitioning Congress for a redress of grievances, or for anything else connected with the powers or duties of the National Government, is an attribute of national citizenship, and, as such, under protection of, and guaranteed by, the United States. The very idea of a government, republican in form, implies a right on the part of its citizens to meet peaceably for consultation in respect to public affairs and to petition for a redress of grievances."

CHAPTER 5

The Way Toward Freedom

You might ask, what does slavery, in all its forms, have to do with rams, ewes, and lambs? Well, I'm glad you asked! You might not like this idea or agree with it, but it is truth: Just as sheep were domesticated by people, so African slaves were domesticated by European Americans. And just as sheep became dependent upon a shepherd, so African slaves became dependent upon European Americans. The same tactics that were used to raise and breed sheep for profit were used to raise and breed African slaves for profit. Just as sheep were treated as property, so African slaves were treated as property, to do with as the slave owners pleased.

Now, I didn't write this book to discuss something that we all already know: Slavery was brutal, cruel, and wrong. But just as the scripture about the sheep to be slaughtered is interpreted with a lack of understanding, so the scriptures about slavery are discussed with a lack of understanding. God never intended for there to be slavery, but He knew that there would be, because of the influence of sin in our lives. So, God gave us guidelines to follow, so that no one would be mistreated. Guidelines that were totally ignored. It's strange how the parts about having slaves in the Bible is discussed, but not the parts about how they were to be treated.

CHAPTER 5

African slaves got their freedom, which was great, but freedom to do what? By the time African slaves were freed, they had come to depend on European American culture, which, at the time, was hostile to those of African descent. So, they were like sheep without a shepherd, wandering aimlessly in a world that they were born into but was not their own. I say wandering aimlessly because these freed slaves were without purpose. Slaves were in America to work and breed, plain and simple. And if this identity had been beaten into you physically, mentally, and spiritually for your whole life, someone telling you you're free is not going to change your identity just like that.

So, those of African descent born in America became American citizens, African Americans. And they struggled and fought, many even died to get to where we are today. And right beside them, even at times daring to take the lead, were some of our most respected, honored, and appreciated European American Brothers and Sisters.

Today, there are African Americans with just as much, and sometimes even more, power and authority than our European American Brothers and Sisters. But how is the power and authority being used? Are the same injustices that were done to those of African descent now being perpetrated by the African Americans? Our African American men and some of our African American women have become drug dealers in their own communities, sex traffickers, murderers of other African Americans, and worse....

Why am I saying these things? To put someone down? Not at all. I haven't been afforded that luxury. I don't have the right nor the want to put anyone down.

I'm saying these things to say that we are all human, with human nature. Power is a dangerous drug. That's why it's so hard to let go of it once you have it. Now just think about ultimate power: The power to do whatever you want with people, whenever you want, however you want. No one should have that kind of power over another human being, much less a whole race of human beings over another race of human beings.

The reason I'm going this route is because God wants us to forgive. God is calling us to a higher place in Him and we won't be able to get into that place with hate in our hearts. Seeing this wasn't always easy for me. It is easier for me now, but only because God has given me understanding of the true fight. Now, of course I still have to stay in God's face because injustice is still going on and I am human as well. It is impossible to see the good that God knows is in people without God's help, especially when they're being unfair to you. But the more I stay in tune with the Holy Spirit and walk this way, the easier it gets. Matthew 9:9 says, "As Jesus went on from there, He saw a man named Matthew (Levi) sitting in the tax collector's booth; and He said to him, 'Follow Me [as My disciple, accepting Me as your Master and Teacher and walking the same path of life that I walk].'"

1 Timothy 2:1-4 says,

> "I urge, first of all, that petitions, prayers, intercession and thanksgiving be made for all people. For kings and all those in authority, that we may live peaceful and quiet lives in all godliness and holiness. This is good, and pleases God our Savior, who wants all people to be saved and to come to a knowledge of the truth."

CHAPTER 5

The Lord wants us to forgive our former oppressors and He also wants the descendants of our former oppressors to forgive themselves. Say what? Yes, this is what God desires: No hate, and no guilt. You would be surprised to know how many of our European American Brothers and Sisters live in bondage in their hearts and minds because of the actions of their ancestors. You might say, good they deserve to be in bondage. True, except we all deserve to be in bondage, that's why God the Father sent His Son Jesus Christ so that we could be free from the bondage of guilt and sin. Romans 1:4 says, "and [as to His divine nature] according to the Spirit of holiness was openly designated to be the Son of God with power [in a triumphant and miraculous way] by His resurrection from the dead: Jesus Christ our Lord."

Ephesians 5:1-2 says,

> "Therefore become imitators of God [copy Him and follow His example], as well-beloved children [imitate their father]; and walk continually in love [that is, value one another, practice empathy and compassion, unselfishly seeking the best for others], just as Christ also loved you and gave Himself up for us, an offering and sacrifice to God [slain for you, so that it became] a sweet fragrance."

Why is it necessary to follow His word? I'm a good person you might say, and everyone is good to some degree, right? Let's see what God tells us in His Word (The Bible).

Ephesians 2:1-5 says,

> "And you [He made alive when you] were [spiritually] dead and separated from Him because of your

transgressions and sins, in which you once walked. You were following the ways of this world [influenced by this present age], in accordance with the prince of the power of the air (Satan), the spirit who is now at work in the disobedient [the unbelieving, who fight against the purposes of God]. Among these [unbelievers] we all once lived in the passions of our flesh [our behavior governed by the sinful self], indulging the desires of human nature [without the Holy Spirit] and [the impulses] of the [sinful] mind.

"We were, by nature, children [under the sentence] of [God's] wrath, just like the rest [of mankind]. But God, being [so very] rich in mercy, because of His great and wonderful love with which He loved us, even when we were [spiritually] dead and separated from Him because of our sins, He made us [spiritually] alive together with Christ (for by His grace, His undeserved favor and mercy, you have been saved from God's judgment). And He raised us up together with Him [when we believed], and seated us with Him in the heavenly places, [because we are] in Christ Jesus, [and He did this] so that in the ages to come He might [clearly] show the immeasurable and unsurpassed riches of His grace in [His] kindness toward us in Christ Jesus [by providing for our redemption].

"For it is by grace [God's remarkable compassion and favor drawing you to Christ] that you have been saved [actually delivered from judgment and given eternal life] through faith. And this [salvation] is not of yourselves [not through your own effort], but it is the [undeserved, gracious] gift of God; not as a result of [your] works [nor your attempts to keep the Law], so that no one will [be able to] boast or take credit in any way [for his salvation]. For we are His workmanship [His own master work, a work of art], created in

Christ Jesus [reborn from above, spiritually transformed, renewed, ready to be used] for good works, which God prepared [for us] beforehand [taking paths which He set], so that we would walk in them [living the good life which He prearranged and made ready for us]."

Answering the Call
Some horrific things have been done and continue to be done. So God is calling everyone, but He will only choose those who answer the call. And in order to answer the call we must do this thing that is impossible on our own, but possible with God.

"You have heard that it was said to the men of old, 'You shall not murder,' and 'Whoever murders shall be guilty before the court.' But I say to you that everyone who continues to be angry with his brother or harbors malice against him shall be guilty before the court; and whoever speaks [contemptuously and insultingly] to his brother, 'Raca (You empty-headed idiot)!' shall be guilty before the supreme court; and whoever says, 'You fool!' shall be in danger of the fiery hell. So, if you are presenting your offering at the altar, and while there you remember that your brother has something [such as a grievance or legitimate complaint] against you, leave your offering there at the altar and go. First make peace with your brother, and then come and present your offering. Come to terms quickly [at the earliest opportunity] with your opponent at law while you are with him on the way [to court], so that your opponent does not hand you over to the judge, and the judge to the guard, and you are thrown into prison. I assure you and most solemnly say to you, you will not come out of there until you have paid the last cent."

Now, God gives us all some responsibility here. To the African American Brothers and Sisters He says, "You have heard that it was said to the men of old, 'You shall not murder,' and 'Whoever murders shall be guilty before the court.' But I say to you that everyone who continues to be angry with his brother or harbors malice against him shall be guilty before the court." And to the European American Brothers and Sisters He says, "So, if you are presenting your offering at the altar, and while there you remember that your brother has something (such as a grievance or legitimate complaint) against you, leave your offering there at the altar and go. First make peace with your brother, and then come and present your offering."

God is not willing to work with us if we have anger or malice in our hearts, and He's not willing to work with us if we have knowingly caused our brothers and sisters to stumble and won't do anything to make it right, just thinking we can go on as if everything is alright.

This is what the forgiveness is all about right here: "Come to terms quickly (at the earliest opportunity) with your opponent at law while you are with him on the way to (court), so that your opponent does not hand you over to the judge, and the judge to the guard, and you are thrown into prison. I assure you and most solemnly say to you, you will not come out of there until you have paid the last cent."

Who is the opponent? Revelations 12:10-12 says,

> "Now the salvation, and the power, and the kingdom (dominion, reign) of our God, and the authority of His Christ have come; for the accuser of our

[believing] brothers and sisters has been thrown down [at last], he who accuses them and keeps bringing charges [of sinful behavior] against them before our God day and night. And they overcame and conquered him because of the blood of the Lamb and because of the word of their testimony, for they did not love their life and renounce their faith even when faced with death (separation from God). Therefore rejoice, O heavens and you who dwell in them [in the presence of God]. Woe to the earth and the sea, because the devil has come down to you in great wrath, knowing that he has only a short time [remaining]!"

The True Fight! We are not each other's enemies. We have a common enemy: Satan! And until we come to grips with that, we'll continue to do Satan's work for him, destroying each other and watching as the world we live in crumbles right before our eyes, not taking into consideration that we are in it.

Let's go to another misunderstanding. Now, I know the Bible calls Satan that "old serpent," but Satan wasn't a serpent (snake), as we know a snake to be. The serpent (snake) allowed Satan to use him to deceive Eve. So, God cursed (empowered to fail) the serpent. Genesis 3:13-14 says,

> "Then the Lord God said to the woman, 'What is this that you have done?' And the woman said, 'The serpent beguiled and deceived me, and I ate [from the forbidden tree].'
>
> "The Lord God said to the serpent, 'Because you have done this, you are cursed more than all the cattle, and more than any animal of the field; On your belly you

shall go, And dust you shall eat all the days of your life.'" Now, we know that Satan is not cattle and he is not an animal of the field."

Let's go to another familiar passage of scripture. John 13:21-27 says,

> "After Jesus had said these things, He was troubled in spirit, and testified and said, 'I assure you and most solemnly say to you, one of you will betray Me and hand Me over.' The disciples began looking at one another, puzzled and disturbed as to whom He could mean. One of His disciples, whom Jesus loved (esteemed), was leaning against Jesus' chest. So, Simon Peter motioned to him (John) and [quietly] asked [him to ask Jesus] of whom He was speaking. Then leaning back against Jesus' chest, he (John) asked Him [privately], 'Lord, who is it?' Jesus answered, 'It is the one to whom I am going to give this piece [of bread] after I have dipped it.' So, when He had dipped the piece of bread [into the dish], He gave it to Judas, son of Simon Iscariot. After [Judas had taken] the piece of bread, Satan entered him. Then Jesus said to him, 'What you are going to do, do quickly [without delay].'"

And one last passage. Genesis 6:5-8,11-12 says,

> "The Lord saw that the wickedness (depravity) of man was great on the earth, and that every imagination or intent of the thoughts of his heart were only evil continually. The Lord regretted that He had made mankind on the earth, and He was [deeply] grieved in His heart. So, the Lord said, 'I will destroy (annihilate) mankind whom I have created from the surface

of the earth, not only man, but the animals and the crawling things and the birds of the air, because it [deeply] grieves Me [to see mankind's sin] and I regret that I have made them.' But Noah found favor and grace in the eyes of the Lord. The [population of the] earth was corrupt [absolutely depraved, spiritually and morally putrid] in God's sight, and the land was filled with violence [desecration, infringement, outrage, assault, and lust for power]. God looked on the earth and saw how debased and degenerate it was, for all humanity had corrupted their way on the earth and lost their true direction."

And what is humanity's true direction? "Father God, Your Kingdom Come, Your Will Be Done On Earth As It Is In Heaven" How? Revelations 12:10-12 says, "Now the salvation, and the power, and the kingdom (dominion, reign) of our God, and the authority of His Christ have come; for the accuser of our [believing] brothers and sisters has been thrown down [at last], he who accuses them and keeps bringing charges [of sinful behavior] against them before our God day and night. And they overcame and conquered him because of the blood of the Lamb and because of the word of their testimony, for they did not love their life and renounce their faith even when faced with death. Therefore rejoice, O heavens and you who dwell in them [in the presence of God]. Therefore rejoice, O Earth and you who dwell in it (in the presence of God)."

Psalms 110:1 says, "The Lord (Father) says to my Lord (the Messiah, His Son), 'Sit at My right hand Until I make Your enemies a footstool for Your feet [subjugating them into complete submission].'"

2 Corinthians 10:4-7 says,

> "The weapons of our warfare are not physical [weapons of flesh and blood]. Our weapons are divinely powerful for the destruction of fortresses. We are destroying sophisticated arguments and every exalted and proud thing that sets itself up against the [true] knowledge of God, and *we are* taking every thought and purpose captive to the obedience of Christ, being ready to punish every act of disobedience, when your own obedience [as The Children of God] is complete. You are looking [only] at the outward appearance of things. If anyone is confident that he is Christ's, he should reflect and consider this, that just as he is Christ's, so too are we."

Galatians 3:28 says,

> "There is [now no distinction in regard to salvation] neither Jew nor Greek, there is neither slave nor free, there is neither male nor female; for you [who believe] are all one in Christ Jesus [no one can claim a spiritual superiority]."

If you can't see Jesus Christ in someone who doesn't have your color skin or is not of your gender, then you'll never be able to see God in His Fullness and you'll never be able to enter His Kingdom.

Just as God took away our ability to unite at the Tower of Babel, he's now giving us the Grace to reunite. Prepare your heart to receive.

Genesis 11:1-9 says,

> "Now the whole earth spoke one language and used the same words (vocabulary). And as people journeyed eastward, they found a plain in the land of Shinar and they settled there. They said one to another,

CHAPTER 5

'Come, let us make bricks and fire them thoroughly [in a kiln, to harden and strengthen them].' So, they used brick for stone [as building material], and they used tar (bitumen, asphalt) for mortar. They said, 'Come, let us build a city for ourselves, and a tower whose top will reach into the heavens, and let us make a [famous] name for ourselves, so that we will not be scattered [into separate groups] and be dispersed over the surface of the entire earth [as the Lord instructed].'

"Now the Lord came down to see the city and the tower which the sons of men had built. And the Lord said, 'Behold, they are one [unified] people, and they all have the same language. This is only the beginning of what they will do [in rebellion against Me], and now no evil thing they imagine they can do will be impossible for them. Come, let Us go down and there confuse and mix up their language, so that they will not understand one another's speech.' So, the Lord scattered them abroad from there over the surface of the entire earth; and they stopped building the city. Therefore, the name of the city was Babel, because there the Lord confused the language of the entire earth; and from that place the Lord scattered and dispersed them over the surface of all the earth."

These were sons of men speaking one common language, and God said because of their unity nothing would be impossible for them, because they believed they could do it. They were together, using the measure of God's Faith, the Gift of God, the very thing God gave us to use for His Glory and bring us to Him, against Him. That's sad! But we are not of that family. God is calling us together and He's Graced us to hear His voice and follow His Word, and as One United Body of Believers We will usher into the earth through His Holy Spirit in the Name, Power, and Authority of Our Lord and Savior Jesus Christ, The Kingdom of God, so that God's Will, will be done on earth as it is in heaven!

CHAPTER 6

Save the Rams

Mal 4:6 says,

"God will turn the hearts of the fathers to their children, and the hearts of the children to their fathers [a reconciliation produced by repentance], so that I will not come and strike the land with a curse [of complete destruction]."

Luke 1:16-17 says,

"He will turn many of the sons of Israel (us, Children of God) back [from sin] to [love and serve] the Lord their God. It is he who will go as a forerunner before Him in the spirit and power of Elijah, to turn the hearts of the fathers back to the children, and the disobedient to the attitude of the righteous [which is to seek and submit to the will of God] in order to make ready a people [perfectly] prepared [spiritually and morally] for the Lord."

We have made major mistakes as men, as husbands, fathers, sons, bosses, friends. Although we have taught from pulpits, we have not taught from the Spirit of God. Our Brothers and Sisters hate each other, fear each other, and have no understanding of each other. That's not

Bible teaching guided by the Holy Spirit. That's carnality, human nature. Our children have to be taught what God's true intention is for this world. It's not that one race or country should have power over everyone else. It's that we must all live together in one world and have submitted (following the leadership and guidance) to God.

This is the misconception: That we have a choice whether we submit to God or not. You are already submitted to God, even if it's in your rebellion.

For a clearer understanding of this, let's take a look at Isaiah 10:1-34. God has empowered the king of Assyria to discipline God's children, for their rebellion against Him. But the king of Assyria doesn't understand that all power and authority is given by God to whomever He wants to give it, for whatever reason He wants to give it to them. In his (the king of Assyria) heart and mind, he (the king of Assyria) is just all powerful and unstoppable. God says,

> "Woe (judgment is coming) to those [judges] who issue evil statutes, and to those [magistrates] who constantly record unjust and oppressive decisions, so as to deprive the needy of justice and rob the poor of My people of rightful claims, so that widows may be their spoil and that they may plunder the fatherless. Now what will you do in the day of [God's] punishment, and in the storm of devastation which will come from far away? To whom will you flee for help? And where will you leave your wealth [for safekeeping]? Nothing remains but to crouch among the captives or fall [dead] among the slain [on the battlefield]."

In spite of all this, God's anger does not turn away, but His hand is still stretched out [in judgment].

"Woe to Assyria, the rod of My anger [against Israel], the staff in whose hand is My indignation and fury [against Israel's disobedience]! I send Assyria against a godless nation
And commission it against the people of My wrath to take the spoil and to seize the plunder, and to trample them down like mud in the streets.

"Yet it is not Assyria's intention [to do My will], nor does it plan so in its heart, but instead it is its purpose to destroy and to cut off many nations. For Assyria says, 'Are not my princes all kings? Is not Calno [conquered] like Carchemish [on the Euphrates]? Is not Hamath [subdued] like Arpad [her neighbor]? Is not Samaria [in Israel] like Damascus [in Aram]? As my hand has reached to the kingdoms of the idols, whose carved images were greater and more feared than those of Jerusalem and Samaria, shall I not do to Jerusalem and her images just as I have done to Samaria and her idols?' [declares Assyria]. So, when the Lord has completed all His work [of judgment] on Mount Zion and on Jerusalem, He will say, 'I will punish the fruit [the thoughts, the declarations, and the actions] of the arrogant heart of the king of Assyria and the haughtiness of his pride.' For the Assyrian king has said, 'I have done this by the power of my [own] hand and by my wisdom, for I have understanding and skill. I have removed the boundaries of the peoples and have plundered their treasures; Like a bull I have brought down those who sat on thrones. My hand has found the wealth of the people like a nest, and as one gathers eggs that are abandoned, so I have gathered all the earth; And there was not one that flapped its wing, or that opened its beak and chirped.

"Is the axe able to lift itself over the one who chops with it? Is the saw able to magnify itself over the one

CHAPTER 6

who wields it? That would be like a club moving those who lift it, or like a staff raising him who is not [made of] wood [like itself]! Therefore, the Lord, the God of hosts, will send a wasting disease among the stout warriors of Assyria; And under his glory a fire will be kindled like a burning flame. And the Light of Israel will become a fire and His Holy One a flame, and it will burn and devour Assyria's thorns and briars in a single day. The Lord will consume the glory of Assyria's Forest and of its fruitful garden, both soul and body, and it will be as when a sick man wastes away. And the remaining trees of Assyria's Forest will be so few in number that a child could write them down.

"Now in that day the remnant of Israel, and those of the house of Jacob who have escaped, will never again rely on the one who struck them, but will truly rely on the Lord, the Holy One of Israel a remnant will return, a remnant of Jacob, to the mighty God. For though your people, O Israel, may be as the sand of the sea, *only* a remnant within them will return; The destruction is determined [it is decided and destined for completion], overflowing with justice (righteous punishment). For the Lord, the God of hosts, will execute a complete destruction, one that is decreed, in the midst of all the land.

"Therefore, the Lord God of hosts says this, 'O My people who dwell in Zion, do not be afraid of the Assyrian who strikes you with a rod and lifts up his staff against you, as [the king of] Egypt did. For yet a very little while and My indignation [against you] will be fulfilled and My anger will be directed toward the destruction of the Assyrian.' The Lord of hosts will brandish a whip against them like the slaughter of Midian at the rock of Oreb; and His staff will be over the [Red] Sea and He will lift it up the way He did in [the flight from] Egypt. So it will be in that day, that the burden of the Assyrian will be removed from your shoulders and his yoke from your neck. The yoke will be broken because of the fat.

"The Assyrian has come against Aiath [in Judah], he has passed through Migron [with his army]; At Michmash he stored his equipment. They have gone through the pass, saying, 'Geba will be our lodging place for the night.' Ramah trembles, and Gibeah [the city] of Saul has fled. Cry aloud with your voice [in consternation], O Daughter of Gallim! Pay attention, Laishah! Answer her, Anathoth! Madmenah has fled; The inhabitants of Gebim have fled [with their belongings] to safety. Yet today the Assyrian will halt at Nob [the city of priests]; He shakes his fist at the mountain of the Daughter of Zion, at the hill of Jerusalem. Listen carefully, the Lord, the God of hosts, will lop off the [beautiful] boughs with terrifying force; The tall in stature will be cut down and the lofty will be abased and humiliated. He will cut down the thickets of the forest with an iron *axe*, and Lebanon (the Assyrian) will fall by the Mighty One."

The Just God
There's been a question floating around in many people's minds. Why does it seem like the righteous are being overtaken by the wicked? I have the answer. Malachi 3:6-7 says, "For I am the Lord, I do not change [but remain faithful to My covenant with you]; that is why you, O sons of Jacob, have not come to an end. Yet from the days of your fathers you have turned away from My

statutes and ordinances and have not kept them. Return to Me, and I will return to you," says the Lord of hosts.

What does that mean? That those who are in Christ Jesus will always be the children of God because that's God's part of the agreement (covenant). But we are not always acting in righteousness (right standing with God), which is just trusting in God and walking according to His purpose for our lives, which is what will turn this mess we're in around. And that's our part of the agreement (covenant) as well.

So, as God's children, God will discipline and correct us sometimes through using those who are rebellious and ruthless, because they won't have a problem carrying out the correction, punishment, or discipline. But what the rebellious don't realize is that it is God's plan to destroy them anyway for their rebellion. He brings them in to correct His children and then He destroys them for correcting His children. Wait, what? No way? Yes way!

You better read your whole Bible. I know you have heard God is Love. Yes, He is Love, but God is a whole lot more than that. He's also Justice and Holiness, and a Just and Holy God will not just sit by and watch His children, as my late grandmother would say, act a fool. Read your Bible. God believes in correcting His children. 1 Corinthians 11:31-32 says, "But if we evaluated and judged ourselves honestly [recognizing our shortcomings and correcting our behavior], we would not be judged. But when we [fall short and] are judged by the Lord, we are disciplined [by undergoing His correction] so that we will not be condemned [to eternal punishment] along with the world."

So, God is not concerned with those who are outside the Body of Christ, at first. God is dealing with His children and once He gets His children straight, then they can go out and make children of everyone who is willing to become a child of God. And let me let you in on a little secret. If you are willing to accept Jesus Christ as your Lord and Personal Savior, it doesn't matter what you've done or what you think you might do after giving your life to Christ.

On the day I gave my life to Jesus Christ, I had a six pack of beer waiting for me in the refrigerator and a football game on my mind. But God was calling me and He wouldn't let up. It wasn't my intention to go to church on that day, but I felt that if I didn't something bad was going to happen, so I went. The best decision I ever made in my life. I got saved that day. I got home and drank three of my beers and...then what? Believe me what happened was good for me. I'm sure the angels were rejoicing. I couldn't finish the other three beers, Hallelujah! Somebody knows why I'm shouting. That was 30 years ago.

God wants you in His family. He always has and He always will. Even if you are one of the rebellious ones He sent to discipline His children. If you say, Lord I repent of (change from) my sins. I don't want to be like this anymore, but I don't know how to change. Help me, please! I accept your Son Jesus Christ into my life as my Lord and Personal Savior and I receive your Holy Spirit into my life to lead and guide me into all truth. Thank You for Your Salvation! I am Redeemed by the Blood of My Lord and Savior Jesus Christ!

Paul wrote the majority of the New Testament portion of the Bible, and he killed Christians prior to being converted. As a matter of fact, when Jesus Called him, he was on his way to Damascus to kill some Christians. He was powerful, just like you, but he was using God's Gift (his power) against God, instead of for God, just like you. (This little piece isn't for everybody, but if God sent it for you, you know.)

Oh, you don't believe it's that easy? Let me give you some scripture. Matthew 9:9-13 says, "As Jesus went on from there, He saw a man named Matthew (Levi) sitting in the tax collector's booth; and He said to him, 'Follow Me [as My disciple, accepting Me as your Master and Teacher and walking the same path of life that I walk].' And Matthew got up and followed Him. Then as Jesus was reclining at the table in Matthew's house, many tax collectors and sinners [including non-observant Jews] came and ate with Him and His disciples. When the Pharisees (religious leaders, teachers of the law) saw this, they asked His disciples, 'Why does your Master eat with tax collectors and sinners?' But when Jesus heard this, He said, 'Those who are healthy have no need for a physician, but [only] those who are sick. Go and learn what this [Scripture] means: "I desire compassion [for those in distress], and not [animal] sacrifice," for I did not come to call [to repentance] the [self-proclaimed] righteous [who see no need to change], but sinners [those who recognize their sin and actively seek forgiveness].'"

Let me give you another one. Luke 18:9-14 says, "He (Jesus) also told this parable to some people who trusted in themselves and were confident that they were righteous [posing outwardly as upright and in right standing with God], and who viewed others with contempt:

"Two men went up into the temple [enclosure] to pray, one a Pharisee and the other a tax collector. The Pharisee stood [ostentatiously] and began praying to himself [in a self-righteous way, saying]: 'God, I thank

You that I am not like the rest of men, swindlers, unjust (dishonest), adulterers, or even like this tax collector. I fast twice a week; I pay tithes of all that I get.' But the tax collector, standing at a distance, would not even raise his eyes toward heaven, but was striking his chest [in humility and repentance], saying, 'God, be merciful and gracious to me, the [especially wicked] sinner [that I am]!' I tell you; this man went to his home justified [forgiven of the guilt of sin and placed in right standing with God] rather than the other man; for everyone who exalts himself will be humbled, but he who humbles himself [forsaking self-righteous pride] will be exalted."

1 Timothy 2:1-8 says, "First of all, then, I urge that petitions (specific requests), prayers, intercessions (prayers for others) and thanksgivings be offered on behalf of all people, for kings and all who are in [positions of] high authority, so that we may live a peaceful and quiet life in all godliness and dignity. This [kind of praying] is good and acceptable and pleasing in the sight of God our Savior, who wishes all people to be saved and to come to the knowledge and recognition of the [divine] truth. For there is [only] one God, and [only] one Mediator between God and mankind, the Man Christ Jesus, who gave Himself as a ransom [a substitutionary sacrifice to atone] for all, the testimony given at the right and proper time. And for this matter I was appointed a preacher and an apostle I am telling the truth, I am not lying [when I say this] a teacher of the Gentiles in faith and truth. Therefore, I want the men in every place to pray, lifting up holy hands, without anger and disputing or quarreling or doubt [in their mind]."

John 17:13-26 says, "But now I (Jesus Christ) am coming to You; and I say these things [while I am still] in the world so that they may experience My joy made full and complete and perfect within them [filling their hearts with My delight]. I have given to them Your word [the message You gave Me]; and the world has hated them because they are not of the world and do not belong to the world, just as I am not of the world and do not belong to it. I do not ask You to take them out of the world, but that You keep them and protect them from the evil one. They are not of the world, just as I am not of the world. Sanctify them in the truth [set them apart for Your purposes, make them holy]; Your word is truth. Just as You commissioned and sent Me into the world, I also have commissioned and sent them (believers) into the world. For their sake I sanctify Myself [to do Your will], so that they also may be sanctified [set apart, dedicated, made holy] in [Your] truth. I do not pray for these alone [it is not for their sake only that I make this request], but also for [all] those who [will ever] believe and trust in Me through their message, that they all may be one; just as You, Father, are in Me and I in You, that they also may be one in Us, so that the world may believe [without any doubt] that You sent Me.

"I have given to them the glory and honor which You have given Me, that they may be one, just as We are one; I in them and You in Me, that they may be perfected and completed into one, so that the world may know [without any doubt] that You sent Me, and [that You] have loved them, just as You have loved Me. Father, I desire that they also, whom You have given to Me [as Your gift to Me], may be with Me where I am, so that they may see My glory which You have given Me, because You loved Me before the foundation of the world. O just *and* righteous Father, although the world has not known

You and has never acknowledged You [and the revelation of Your mercy], yet I have always known You; and these [believers] know [without any doubt] that You sent Me; and I have made Your name known to them, and will continue to make it known, so that the love with which You have loved Me may be in them [overwhelming their heart], and I [may be] in them."

The Choice is Ours
When Adam and Eve ate from the tree of the knowledge of good and evil they hid themselves from God because of their shame. "I was naked" Adam said to God, "and who told you, you were naked?" God asked, did you eat from the tree I told you not to?"

The tree of the knowledge of good and evil gives us choice. The choice between right and wrong, good and evil, God and Satan. And the knowing of good and evil brings responsibility. The responsibility to choose. The Bible says Satan made accusations of sin to God about our brothers in heaven day and night. But they overcame by the word of their testimony and the blood of the Lamb.

So, we first get a picture of our lives through Adam and Eve without the influence of Satan (the tree of the knowledge of good and evil). They had no choice, they just did what God told them to do. Much like children before they hit their teenage years, lol. Satan knows good and evil. And what is evil? Evil is the choice to walk outside of the way God has chosen (ordained) for your life. Satan knows how to walk in God's ways and he knows how to rebel against God's ways. He has chosen to rebel against God's ways and his hope/plan is to deceive as many as he can into doing the same.

CHAPTER 6

The Bible says they (Adam and Eve) heard the Lord walking in the garden and they hid themselves, but the Lord said, "Adam Where are you?" Adam said to God "I heard you walking in the garden, and I was afraid because I was naked." Now, remember right before this encounter, Adam and Eve had sewn fig leaves together to make coverings for themselves. So, although they felt covered before each other, they were still naked before God. So, when we're out here trying to act one way or another before people, the only one who really matters already knows who we are. He made us, He loves us and He knows what it's going to take to get us from where we are to where He wants us to be. But we first have to be honest with ourselves about where we are. And to walk with God you have to continuously change (grow).

So, if you think you are already where you need to be and you don't have any more growing to do, that's where you need to start your change (growing). Through every generation from Adam and Eve until the present day, "the knowledge of good and evil" has been passed down. Good! (Seek ye first the Kingdom of God; Not my will, but your will be done; Your Kingdom come, Your Will be done on earth as it is in Heaven.)

Evil says, "I did it my way." No disrespect to the Legend, Frank Sinatra. A beautiful song and beautifully sung. But I needed to use his wording. If you did it your way (without God's instruction), unless God intervened for the benefit of His Will, you did it Satan's way.

From day one, mankind, God's creation, has chosen Satan over God. And not choosing is a choice as well. In Matthew 12:30, Jesus says, "He who is not with Me [once and for all on My side] is against Me; and he who does not [unequivocally] gather with Me scatters."

Why is this so cut and dry? Why does Jesus make this statement? Because there are only two sides. You are born into one, sin and Satan, and you must choose the other, God (The Father, The Son, and The Holy Spirit). You must confess Jesus as your Lord and personal Savior.

Romans 5:18-21 says, "So then as through one trespass [Adam's sin] there resulted condemnation for all men, even so through one act of righteousness there resulted justification of life to all men. For just as through one man's disobedience [his failure to hear, his carelessness] the many were made sinners, so through the obedience of the one Man the many will be made righteous and acceptable to God and brought into right standing with Him. But the Law came to increase and expand [the awareness of] the trespass [by defining and unmasking sin]. But where sin increased, [God's remarkable, gracious gift of] grace [His unmerited favor] has surpassed it and increased all the more, so that, as sin reigned in death, so also grace would reign through righteousness which brings eternal life through Jesus Christ our Lord."

You might say, this doesn't seem fair. Why do we have to go through all of this for something Adam and Eve did? Good question! I have a question, as well. Why should God have to go through another rebellion (war) on earth like the one that was in heaven?

Let's take a look at how amazing God is. And, as my fingers work to type the remarkable ways of God, I can barely contain myself. I stand in Awe!!! Remember, I showed you how God uses who He wants, when He wants, how He wants. That includes Satan. See, there was another tree in the middle of the garden. Do you know what it was? Yes, the Tree of Life. If Adam and Eve had eaten from the Tree of Life they would have lived forever, and God never forbade them from eating from the Tree of Life. So, why didn't Satan tell them to eat from the Tree of Life so they could live forever? Because he didn't want them to live. He wanted the same thing for them as he wants for you and me, for us to die (be separated from God).

Let's take a closer look: Two trees in the middle of the garden, two choices, two totally different directions. Does this sound familiar? Yes. The tree of the knowledge of good and evil brings death (separation from God forever), Satan, while the Tree of Life brings Eternal Life with God. John 17:1-3 says, "When Jesus had spoken these things, He raised His eyes to heaven [in prayer] and said, 'Father, the hour has come. Glorify Your Son, so that Your Son may glorify You. Just as You have given Him power and authority over all mankind, [now glorify Him] so that He may give eternal life to all whom You have given Him [to be His permanently and forever]. Now this is eternal life: that they may know You, the only true [supreme and sovereign] God, and [in the same manner know] Jesus [as the] Christ whom You have sent.'"

Genesis 3:22 says, "And the Lord God said, 'Behold, the man has become like one of Us, knowing [how to distinguish between] good and evil; and now, he might stretch out his hand, and take from the tree of life as well, and eat [its fruit], and live [in this fallen, sinful condition] forever.'"

Revelation 2:7 says, "He who has an ear, let him hear and heed what the Spirit says to the churches. To him who overcomes [the world through believing that Jesus is the Son of God], I will grant [the privilege] to eat [the fruit] from the tree of life, which is in the Paradise of God."

Revelation 22:1-5 says, "Then the angel showed me a river of the water of life, clear as crystal, flowing from the throne of God and of the Lamb (Christ), in the middle of its street. On either side of the river was the tree of life, bearing twelve kinds of fruit, yielding its fruit every month; and the leaves of the tree were for the healing of the nations. There will no longer exist anything that is cursed [because sin and illness and death are gone]; and the throne of God and of the Lamb will be in it, and His bondservants will serve and worship Him [with great awe and joy and loving devotion]; they will [be privileged to] see His face, and His name will be on their foreheads. And there will no longer be night; they have no need for lamplight or sunlight, because the Lord God will illumine them; and they will reign [as kings] forever and ever."

From day one, God's creation (mankind) has chosen not to follow God. No matter how much God blesses us; no matter how much we suffer. Matthew 11:17-19 says, "But to what shall I compare this generation? It is like little children sitting in the market places, who call to the others, and say 'We piped the flute for you [playing wedding], and you did not dance; we wailed sad dirges [playing funeral], and you did not mourn and cry aloud.' For John came neither eating nor drinking [with others], and they say, 'He has a demon!' The Son of Man came eating and drinking [with others], and they say, 'Look! A glutton and a drunkard, a friend of tax collectors and sinners [including non-observant Jews]!' We refuse to repent (change)."

CHAPTER 6

We don't take the time God has given us as a blessing. We say, where is this Jesus you talk so much about, what's taking Him so long? What, does He need a GPS, does He need to ask Alexa or Siri how to get back? Yeh, funny.

2 Peter 3:1-9 says, "Beloved, I am now writing you this second letter. In this [as in the first one], I am stirring up your untainted mind to remind you, that you should remember the words spoken in the past [about the future] by the holy prophets and the commandment of the Lord and Savior given by your apostles [His personally chosen representatives]. First of all, know [without any doubt] that mockers will come in the last days with their mocking, following after their own human desires and saying, 'Where is the promise of His coming [what has become of it]? For ever since the fathers fell asleep [in death], all things have continued [exactly] as they did from the beginning of creation.' For they willingly forget [the fact] that the heavens existed long ago by the word of God, and the earth was formed out of water and by water, through which the world at that time was destroyed by being flooded with water. But by His word the present heavens and earth are being reserved for fire, being kept for the day of judgment and destruction of the ungodly people.' Nevertheless, do not let this one *fact* escape your notice, beloved, that with the Lord one day is like a thousand years, and a thousand years is like one day. The Lord does not delay [as though He were unable to act] and is not slow about His promise, as some count slowness, but is [extraordinarily] patient toward you, not wishing for any to perish but for all to come to repentance."

Which is to say that, after all the time God has patiently waited for us, He only wants the best for us. And His way is best for us. The world was created by Him. So, it shouldn't be hard to understand that the world is designed to operate by His format, and if you use another format, you'll eventually ruin the world.

Genesis 3:17 says it this way: "Then to Adam the Lord God said, 'Because you have listened [attentively] to the voice of your wife, and have eaten [fruit] from the tree about which I commanded you, saying, "You shall not eat of it;" The ground is [now] under a curse (empowered to fail) because of you; In sorrow and toil you shall eat [the fruit] of it All the days of your life.'"

Why? Why is the ground under a curse (empowered to fail)? Proverbs 14:12 says, "There is a way which seems right to a man and appears straight before him, but its end is the way of death." What we do in the world when we are apart from God's Will seems good, but it won't end good. And no matter how mad and rebellious we get, it won't change the fact that no matter how smart you think you are, you don't know what you're doing. Figuring out God's design is way above your pay grade. God's design can't be figured out, it can only be revealed, by, guess who? Yes, that's right, you guessed it, God.

Romans 8:18-25 says, "For I consider [from the standpoint of faith] that the sufferings of the present life are not worthy to be compared with the glory that is about to be revealed to us and in us! For [even the whole] creation [all nature] waits eagerly for the children of God to be revealed. For the creation was subjected to frustration and futility, not willingly [because of some intentional fault on its part], but by the will of Him who subjected it, in hope that the creation itself will also be freed from its bondage to decay [and gain entrance] into the glorious freedom of the children of God. For we know that the whole creation has been moaning together as in the pains of childbirth until now. And not only this, but we too, who have the first fruits of the Spirit [a joyful indication of the blessings to come], even we groan inwardly, as we wait eagerly for [the sign of] our adoption as sons, the redemption and transformation of our body. For in this hope we were saved [by faith]. But hope [the object of] which is seen is not hope. For who hopes for what he already sees? But if we hope for what we do not see, we wait eagerly for it with patience and composure."

Let me sum this up: Satan tried to take over heaven with his evil tactics and he was able to deceive 1/3 of the angels in heaven to side with him. A war broke out and Satan and the angels he deceived lost their places in heaven and were cast down to the earth. God created mankind, so Satan figured, let me take a crack at God's Creation.

Now remember, Satan can't do anything unless God gives him permission. So, when God says it's not good for man to be alone and he puts man to sleep and pulls the female out of the side of Man, I am not surprised. See, man was not alone in the garden, man had God. Man was a spiritual being in the garden, man could relate to God. But because man wasn't going to be in the garden anymore, man had to be able to pro-create. In comes Satan. Or, to put it another way, in comes choice.

God wants us to love Him, not because we have to, but because we want to. So, choose. There are two trees in the middle of the garden, one God tells them (and us) not to touch the other God says nothing about.

Obviously, their minds were free to choose, they just didn't have a choice. But when given a choice, God's children chose against Him.

If you go back over the creation story in Genesis chapters 1 and 2 you'll see that after God created something "it was good." There was no evil. So, until Satan introduced them to it Adam and Eve had no knowledge of evil. No choice.

Genesis 3:22 says, And the LORD God said, "The man has now become like one of us, knowing good and evil. He must not be allowed to reach out his hand and take also from the tree of life and eat and live forever (in this condition of sin)."

Why do you think we have families? So through them we can understand God's will. Romans 1:20 says, "For ever since the creation of the world His invisible attributes, His eternal power and divine nature, have been clearly seen, being understood through His workmanship [all His creation, the wonderful things that He has made], so that they [who fail to believe and trust in Him] are without excuse and without defense."

God created family. Remember when your child was still at home with you and she was your little sweetheart, and then she started school and started getting on social media and started making friends and one day you didn't know who this person was in your house, where did they come from? Does this sound familiar: "I've got to do me mom" or "I'm just keeping it real dad" or "I'm just keeping it 100%".

How do you feel when you have charted a path for your child that will give them a great, safe life, and they go in the total opposite direction? When you can see the destruction of their life and everything they come in contact with before it even happens? You are, after all, the parent and you know where the road they're on leads better than they do. Except you're really just *hoping* that your way works, because you don't have total control of life, you're just human and things happen.

But God, on the other hand, knows exactly what way is best for you and He does have total control. So it will work, His way, without a doubt, and not just for you. God's purpose and plan for all of us is to help each other. It's not just about you. God didn't give you all those gifts and talents just for you and yours. How do you think God feels when you act selfishly? If you become angry and upset and your only concern is you and yours, how do you think God should feel when His concern is everything and everybody?

So, Eve listened to Satan and Adam listened to Eve and they were all thrown out of the garden. Why were they put out of the garden? Because of their choice! But God loves us so much and God is so beyond wise that He was already prepared for this. I would even be so bold as to say that God planned the whole thing.

Our Mortal Body
1 Corinthians 15:42-50 says, "So it is with the resurrection of the dead. The [human] body that is sown is perishable and mortal, it is raised imperishable and immortal. It is sown in dishonor, it is raised in glory; it is sown in weakness, it is raised in strength; it is sown a natural body [mortal, suited to earth], it is raised a spiritual body [immortal, suited to heaven]. As surely as there is a physical body, there is also a spiritual body. So, it is written [in Scripture], 'The first man, Adam, became a living soul (an individual); the last Adam (Christ) became a

life-giving spirit [restoring the dead to life]. However, the spiritual [the immortal life] is not first, but the physical [the mortal life]; then the spiritual.

"'The first man [Adam] is from the earth, earthy [made of dust]; the second Man [Christ, the Lord] is from heaven. As is the earthly man [the man of dust], so are those who are of earth; and as is the heavenly [Man], so are those who are of heaven. Just as we have borne the image of the earthly [the man of dust], we will also bear the image of the heavenly [the Man of heaven]. Now I say this, believers, that flesh and blood cannot inherit nor be part of the kingdom of God; nor does the perishable (mortal) inherit the imperishable (immortal).'"

Man is a Spirit, but God wrapped man in something perishable. I know David said, "I am fearfully and wonderfully made," and this is true, but compared to our real (heavenly) bodies, there is no comparison. So, Satan has control of nothing, nothing permanent. These bodies are not meant to last, this world is not meant to last.

Now, don't get me wrong. I'm going to take care of my earthy body and pray for strength and good health for as long as I'm in this world, and yes, I consider myself fearfully and wonderfully made as well. But comparing this body with our heavenly body is like comparing this heaven and earth with the new heaven and earth (The New Jerusalem). This body was created for destruction, just as this present heaven and earth was created to be destroyed by fire.

Philippians 3:3 says, "for we [who are born again have been reborn from above, spiritually transformed, renewed, set apart for His purpose and] are the true circumcision, who worship in the Spirit of God and glory and take pride and exult in Christ Jesus and place no confidence [in what we have or who we are] in the flesh."

Does this mean we shouldn't take care of what we are and who we are in the world? Of course not! We are to be good stewards over everything God has blessed us with, including our talents and abilities. But we aren't to be consumed with them. We understand that everything we have and everything we are is for the advancement of God's Kingdom in the earth and everything we are and everything we have is because of God's favor in our lives.

Solomon said it this way: "it's all vanity, a chasing after the wind." Why did he say this? Because it's all temporary! Why would you give your allegiance to a way of life that will only last for your time on this earth? Okay, you say, I want to ball out and this is the way I have to live to do that. So, you ball out for 70, 80, 90, 100 years and then you die and suffer for all eternity.

I hear you, you ask, "What if I'm wrong about eternal suffering?" Well, if I'm wrong, then all you did was live as is reported in Micah 6:8: "He (God) has told you, O man, what is good; And what does the Lord require of you except to be just, and to love [and to diligently practice] kindness (compassion), And to walk humbly with your God [setting aside any overblown sense of importance or self-righteousness]?"

That's If I'm wrong. **BUT WHAT IF I'M RIGHT!?!**

Satan's Way, or God's?

So, the father gave His son Jesus Christ so that whoever believes in Him will not perish but will have eternal life.

This is the deal when we were in the garden and God gave us everything: We chose Satan's way. This is just like the prodigal son, who had everything, but chose to leave his father, because he wanted to ball out. What he didn't realize is that he could lose everything balling out, but that's what happened, he lost his whole inheritance. Just as we lost our relationship with God and the Garden of Eden.

Luke 15:11-24 says,

> "Then He said, 'A certain man had two sons. The younger of them [inappropriately] said to his father, "Father, give me the share of the property that falls to me." So, he divided the estate between them. A few days later, the younger son gathered together everything [that he had] and traveled to a distant country, and there he wasted his fortune in reckless and immoral living. Now when he had spent everything, a severe famine occurred in that country, and he began to do without and be in need. So, he went and forced himself on one of the citizens of that country, who sent him into his fields to feed pigs. He would have gladly eaten the [carob] pods that the pigs were eating [but they could not satisfy his hunger], and no one was giving anything to him. But when he [finally] came to his senses, he said, "'How many of my father's hired men have more than enough food, while I am dying here of hunger! I will get up and go to my father, and I will say to him, 'Father, I have sinned against heaven and in your sight. I am no longer worthy to be called your son; [just] treat me like one of your hired men.' So, he got up and came to his father. But while he was still a long way off, his father saw him and was moved with compassion for him and ran and embraced him and kissed him. And the son said to him, "Father, I have sinned against heaven and in your sight; I am no longer worthy to be called your son." But the father said to his servants, "Quickly

bring out the best robe [for the guest of honor] and put it on him; and give him a ring for his hand, and sandals for his feet. And bring the fattened calf and slaughter it and let us [invite everyone and] feast and celebrate; for this son of mine was [as good as] dead and is alive again; he was lost and has been found." So, they began to celebrate.'"

The story of the prodigal son is the whole Gospel in one parable. The prodigal son chose to live outside the will of his father. But the father never lost love for his son, so when the son saw that the world wasn't good for him and it wasn't actually his friend, the Bible says he came to himself. He remembered he was the son of a king, and he shouldn't be allowing himself to be treated less than who he truly is, by treating *himself* less than who he truly is. So, he was humbled by his experience in the world, and, in his humility, he found himself and he understood: "I have sinned against heaven and I have sinned against my father I don't even deserve to be called his son, but I'll ask him to let me back in as a servant." He repented (changed). He said this to his father and his father threw a celebration for his return.

We started in sin (a choice) with Adam and Eve, but we can all return by humbly accepting for our lives the sacrifice of our Lord and Savior Jesus Christ (a choice).

I feel I need to add this: It doesn't matter how many sins you have committed or how few you have committed. It doesn't matter how severe the sin or how minor in action. It's all the same to God.

Romans 3:21-26 says, "But now the righteousness of God has been clearly revealed [independently and completely] apart from the Law, though it is [actually] confirmed by the Law and the [words and writings of the]

Prophets. This righteousness of God comes through faith in Jesus Christ for all those [Jew or Gentile] who believe [and trust in Him and acknowledge Him as God's Son]. There is no distinction, since all have sinned and continually fall short of the glory of God, and are being justified [declared free of the guilt of sin, made acceptable to God, and granted eternal life] as a gift by His [precious, undeserved] grace, through the redemption [the payment for our sin] which is [provided] in Christ Jesus, whom God displayed publicly [before the eyes of the world] as a [life-giving] sacrifice of atonement and reconciliation (propitiation) by His blood [to be received] through faith. This was to demonstrate His righteousness [which demands punishment for sin], because in His forbearance [His deliberate restraint] He passed over the sins previously committed [before Jesus' crucifixion]. It was to demonstrate His righteousness at the present time, so that He would be just and the One who justifies those who have faith in Jesus [and rely confidently on Him as Savior]."

Where am I going with this? The older brother of the prodigal son was angry with his father for receiving the father's son and his younger brother back into the family. But in the father's eyes, the prodigal son was never out of the family.

Luke 25:25-32 says,

> "Now his older son was in the field; and when he returned and approached the house, he heard music and dancing. So, he summoned one of the servants and began asking what this [celebration] meant. And he said to him, 'Your brother has come, and your father has killed the fattened calf because he has received him back safe and sound.' But the elder

brother became angry and deeply resentful and was not willing to go in; and his father came out and began pleading with him.

"But he said to his father, 'Look! These many years I have served you, and I have never neglected or disobeyed your command. Yet you have never given me [so much as] a young goat, so that I might celebrate with my friends; but when this [other] son of yours arrived, who has devoured your estate with immoral women, you slaughtered that fattened calf for him!' The father said 'rejoice, for this brother of yours was [as good as] dead and has begun to live. He was lost and has been found.'"

So, instead of being happy to celebrate his younger brothers return, the older brother was upset. Why? Because the older brother felt that since he had been obedient to the father, by doing everything the father told him to do (kept the law), he should be favored. I'm not certain he kept the law completely, but even if he did, so what? That doesn't give him the right to keep another son out of his father's house. The older brother is a son as well, not the father. He's not in charge. It's The Father's House!

Ephesians 2:8-9 says,

"For it is by grace [God's remarkable compassion and favor drawing you to Christ] that you have been saved [actually delivered from judgment and given eternal life] through faith. And this [salvation] is not of yourselves [not through your own effort], but it is the [undeserved, gracious] gift of God; not as a result of [your] works [nor your attempts to keep the Law], so that no one will [be able to] boast or take credit in any way [for his salvation]."

So, no one is in the Father's house because they've worked their way in. Everyone that is in, is in because the Holy Spirit drew them in by the Grace of God. And if God's Grace drew you in before someone else, be thankful that God showed them the same Love and compassion that He showed you.

CHAPTER 6

Conclusion

Okay, let's see if we can wrap this up.
First let me explain to you why I use the terms African American and European American instead of black people and white people. It's simple: Because we are not crayons and I've never actually seen a white person. The closest I've seen is the albino man in the movie *Powder*. I know that those who call themselves white are of European descent but there is an issue involved with using color in this manner.

In the African American, culture there is the question of complexion. There are many complexions within that culture. When you use black to describe the whole race, everyone is looking to see who is the closest to the color of black so that they can determine who is or isn't a part of the race. But with "African American," it doesn't matter what your complexion is, the only thing that matters is that you are of African ancestry.

See we all migrated to America. Some freely, some forcibly, but we all came to America from somewhere else. Except of course our Native American Brothers and Sisters. Now if anyone could be called Americans, it would be our Indigenous Brothers and Sisters, whom I call Native Americans because they are the only ones who are Native to this land called America.

CHAPTER 6

History of the Native Americans and the Early European Americans

Let me give you a little more Native history:

For thousands of years, North America was populated mainly by Native Americans and was mostly unknown to Europe. In the 1500s, Europeans began arriving in North America; they found a land with many natural resources and began to claim parts of it. As the French moved into the north and the Spanish settled in the south and west, the British founded colonies on the east coast.

The British settlers came to these new lands for many reasons. Some wanted to make money or set up trade with their home country while others wanted religious freedom. In the early 1600s, the British king began establishing colonies in America. By the 1700s, most of the settlements had formed into 13 British colonies: Connecticut, Delaware, Georgia, Maryland, Massachusetts, New Hampshire, New York, New Jersey, Virginia, North Carolina, Pennsylvania, Rhode Island, and South Carolina.

The colonists, or people living in the colonies, were unhappy about paying taxes without having any say in their government. This unhappiness would eventually lead to a clash between the Americans and the British, which would then lead to the American Revolutionary War (1775-1783). When the British were defeated at the end of the war, America was free to take the first steps toward creating a new system of government.

Before the American Revolutionary War, each state had its own constitution, which gave people certain rights, such as freedom of speech, religion, and the press. During the war, the 13 colonies united to free themselves from British rule. The states were very different from each other, but they realized that, in order to grow and prosper, they needed to form a union.

The states joined together to set up a central government. Delegates from each state met and a plan for unity was initially submitted at the Second Continental Congress on July 12, 1776. After much debate, on November 15, 1777, the states finally established a "firm league of friendship" that became known as the Articles of Confederation. The Articles, however, did not go into effect until March 1, 1781.

In September of 1786, there was a meeting in Annapolis, Maryland where representatives from New York, New Jersey, Delaware, Virginia, and Pennsylvania met to see what they could do about trade problems among the states. As time passed it became clear that changes to this system of government had to be made.

God's Way and the American Way

Why am I discussing politics in a book about God? As I stated, Evil is anything apart from God's Will and Purpose and the fruit of evil is sin. Good is God's Will and Purpose and the fruit of that good is life with God. If you choose to separate a whole country, especially one as powerful as America from the Will of God, you are choosing to spread evil (Satan) all around the world, because America of course has that much God-given influence, authority, and power. But if you choose to invite God into your country, especially one with as much God-given power, authority, and influence as America (which in my opinion, even with its shortcomings, which all countries have, is the greatest country in the world), you are choosing to spread good (God) all around the world.

CHAPTER 6

And I say "invite" because God won't force himself on us individually or as a country. Romans 13:1 says, "Let every person be subject to the governing authorities. For there is no authority except from God [granted by His permission and sanction], and those which exist have been put in place by God."

When I run across a scripture like this, it makes me wonder, does God know what's going on in the world? And my answer is yes, I know He does. So what is the deal? Should we, as children of God, involve ourselves in politics?

Okay, here it is. I've heard children of God say, stay out of politics, it's evil, it'll take you down a terrible road, you have to be corrupt to be a politician. But as you took this journey with me, did you not notice that everything I discussed here was dictated from the top, the government? All of the rules I wrote about, all the regulations, both those that were good and evil, just and fair, righteous or corrupt.

So, how can we make anything better, turn anything around, give God control of the country, if we're afraid to accept the very political positions that are designed by God to do just that? There are only two sides, God and Satan, and neither of them is going to fill out a job application or run for office. So, if the children of God refuse to receive and take the positions of power, authority, and influence that were designed by God for them, who's left?

Why do I say that these positions were designed for the children of God, you might ask?

Romans 13:1-7 says, "Let every person be subject to the governing authorities. For there is no authority except from God [granted by His permission and sanction], and those which exist have been put in place by

God. Therefore, whoever resists [governmental] authority resists the ordinance of God. And those who have resisted it will bring judgment (civil penalty) on themselves. For [civil] authorities are not a source of fear for [people of] good behavior, but for [those who do] evil. Do you want to be unafraid of authority? Do what is good and you will receive approval and commendation. For he is God's servant to you for good. But if you do wrong, [you should] be afraid; for he does not carry the [executioner's] sword for nothing. He is God's servant, an avenger who brings punishment on the wrongdoer. Therefore, one must be subject [to civil authorities], not only to escape the punishment [that comes with wrongdoing], but also as a matter of principle [knowing what is right before God]. For this same reason you pay taxes, for civil authorities are God's servants, devoting themselves to governance. Pay to all what is due: tax to whom tax is due, customs to whom customs, respect to whom respect, honor to whom honor."

Who other than a child of God, someone with God's Spirit dwelling on the inside of them, would God want to give this much authority, power, influence, and responsibility?

We ask God for help, but when God gives it, we don't recognize it because we don't understand that we have a hand in the help we're asking for. Ephesians 2:10 says, "For we are His workmanship [His own master work, a work of art], created in Christ Jesus [reborn from above, spiritually transformed, renewed, ready to be used] for good works, which God prepared [for us] beforehand [taking paths which He set], so that we would walk in them [living the good life which He prearranged and made ready for us]."

CHAPTER 6

Romans 8:36-39 says, "Just as it is written and forever remains written,

"For Your sake we are put to death all day long; We are regarded as sheep for the slaughter."

Yet in all these things we are more than conquerors and gain an overwhelming victory through Him who loved us [so much that He died for us]. For I am convinced [and continue to be convinced beyond any doubt] that neither death, nor life, nor angels, nor principalities, nor things present and threatening, nor things to come, nor powers, nor height, nor depth, nor any other created thing, will be able to separate us from the [unlimited] love of God, which is in Christ Jesus our Lord."

Isaiah 41:10 says, "Do not fear [anything], for I am with you; Do not be afraid, for I am your God. I will strengthen you, be assured I will help you; I will certainly take hold of you with My righteous right hand [a hand of justice, of power, of victory, of salvation]."

Don't wait for difference to come! UR the difference!! UR Ministry In Action!!!

References

Bancroft, Frederic (1931). *Slave Trading in the Old South*. Columbia, SC: University of South Carolina Press.

Becker, Carl L. (1970) [1922]. *The Declaration of Independence: A Study in the History of Political Ideas* (Revised ed.). New York: Vintage Books.

Berlin, Ira. *Many Thousands Gone: The First Two Centuries of Slavery in North America*, Cambridge, MA: The Belknap Press of Harvard University Press, 1998.

Bright, Ashleigh. "The short scrotum method of castration in lambs: a review" (PDF). FAI Farms Ltd.

Brown, Dave; Meadowcroft, Sam (1996). *The Modern Shepherd*. Ipswich, United Kingdom: Farming Press.

Brown, Richard D. (2017). *Self-evident truths: contesting equal rights from the Revolution to the Civil War*. New Haven.

Carlson, Alvar Ward. "New Mexico's Sheep Industry: 1850–1900, Its Role in the History of the Territory." New Mexico Historical Review 44.1 (1969).

Davis, David Brion (2014). "Slavery, Sex, and Dehumanization." In Gwyn Campbell and Elizabeth Elbourne's Sex, Power, and Slavery. Athens, OH: Ohio University Press.

Donoghue, Eddie Black *Breeding Machines: The Breeding of Negro Slaves in the Diaspora*, Author House, 2008.

Dube, Ann Marie (May 1996). "The Declaration of Independence". A Multitude of Amendments, Alterations and Additions: The Writing and Publicizing of the Declaration of Independence, the Articles of Confederation, and the Constitution of the United States. National Park Service. Archived from the original on November 8, 2012. Retrieved July 1, 2011.

Ellis, Joseph (2007). *American Creation: Triumphs and Tragedies at the Founding of the Republic*. New York: Knopf.

Ferling, John. *Setting the World Ablaze: Washington, Adams, Jefferson, and the American Revolution*, Oxford University Press.

Finkelman, Paul and Joseph C. Miller, eds. (1998). Macmillan *Encyclopedia of World Slavery, Vol. 2*. New York: Simon & Schuster.

Fogel, Robert; Engerman, Stanley (1995). *Time on the Cross: The Economics of American Negro Slavery*. New York: Norton.

Galenson, David. *Traders, Planters, and Slaves: Market Behavior in Early English America*, 1986.

Hornsby, Alton Jr. (2011) *Black America: A State-by-State Historical Encyclopedia*. Santa Barbara CA: Greenwood Press.

Jensen, Merrill (1968). *The Founding of a Nation: A History of the American Revolution, 1763–1776*. New York: Oxford University Press.

Jones, Keithly G. "Trends in the US sheep industry" (USDA Economic Research Service, 2004).

Kolchin, Peter. *American Slavery, 1619–1877* (1993).

REFERENCES

Maier, Pauline (1997). *American Scripture: Making the Declaration of Independence*. New York: Knopf.

Marable, Manning (2000). *How Capitalism Underdeveloped Black America: Problems in Race, Political Economy, and Society*. Boston: South End Press.

Mead, John (2008). "Declarations of Liberty: Representations of Black/White Alliances Against Slavery by John Brown, James Redpath, and Thomas Wentworth Higginson". Journal for the Study of Radicalism. 3 (1): 111–144.

Merriam-Webster online Archived April 24, 2009, at the Wayback Machine; Dictionary.com Archived April 9, 2009, at the Wayback Machine.

Miller, John and Smith, David (1988). *Dictionary of Afro-American Slavery*. Westport, CT: Greenwood Press.

Minto, John. "Sheep Husbandry in Oregon. The Pioneer Era of Domestic Sheep Husbandry." The Quarterly of the Oregon Historical Society (1902).

Monbiot, George (October 2013). *Feral - Rewilding the land, sea and human life*.

Perkins, John. "Up the Trail From Dixie: Animosity Toward Sheep in the Culture of the US West." Australasian Journal of American Studies (1992).

Reid, John "The Irrelevance of the Declaration," in Hendrik Hartog, ed., Law in the American Revolution and the Revolution in the Law (New York University Press, 1981).

Schneider, Dorothy and Carl J. Schneider (2000). *Slavery in America from Colonial Times to the Civil War*. New York: Facts on File.

Sutch, Richard. "The Breeding of Slaves for Sale and the Westward Expansion of Slavery, 1850–1860," in Stanley L. Engerman and Eugene Genovese (eds), Race and Slavery in the Western Hemishpere: Q Studies, Princeton University Press, 1975.

Sublette, Ned and Constance Sublette (2016). *American Slave Coast: A History of the Slave-Breeding Industry.* Chicago, Illinois: Chicago Review Press.

"TeachAmericanHistory.org: John Hancock" (PDF). Archived from the original (PDF) on May 10, 2013. Retrieved October 6, 2014.

Wills, Gary. Inventing America: *Jefferson's Declaration of Independence* Archived September 26, 2015, at the Wayback Machine, (Houghton Mifflin Harcourt, 2002): "the Declaration is not a legal instrument, like the Constitution".

Witherell, William H. "A comparison of the determinants of wool production in the six leading producing countries: 1949–1965." American Journal of Agricultural Economics 51.1 (1969).

Wypijewski, JoAnn (May 2022). *The Long Hand of Slave Breeding*, Redux. In Counterpunch.

"Abraham Lincoln (1809–1865): Political Debates Between Lincoln and Douglas 1897." Bartleby. Archived from the original on May 10, 2013. Retrieved January 26, 2013.

A New Birth of Freedom: Abraham Lincoln and the Coming of the Civil War (2000).

College of Agriculture and Home Economics. "Sheep Production and Management" (PDF).

"Declaration of Independence: A Transcription". National Archives. November 1, 2015. Archived from the original on July 6, 2019. Retrieved July 6, 2019.

REFERENCES

"History of Wool." The Big Merino. Retrieved 2019-08-30.

"The Contagion of Sovereignty: Declarations of Independence since 1776" (PDF). Archived (PDF) from the original on September 16, 2012. Retrieved August 17, 2012.

"The suffering of farmed sheep." Animal Aid. Retrieved 2019-06-04.

"The Three Greatest Men." Library of Congress. Archived from the original on June 1, 2009. Retrieved June 13, 2009. Jefferson identified Bacon, Locke, and Newton as "the three greatest men that have ever lived, without any exception." Their works in the physical and moral sciences were instrumental in Jefferson's education and world view.

"Welfare group targets abuse in Australian shearing sheds." ABC News. 10 July 2014. Retrieved 17 September 2014.

Wills, *Inventing America*, especially chps. 11–13. Wills concludes (p. 315) that "the air of enlightened America was full of Hutcheson's politics, not Locke's." Hamowy, "Jefferson and the Scottish Enlightenment," argues that Wills gets much wrong (p. 523), that the Declaration seems to be influenced by Hutcheson because Hutcheson was, like Jefferson, influenced by Locke (pp. 508–09), and that Jefferson often wrote of Locke's influence, but never mentioned Hutcheson in any of his writings.

Work Projects Administration, *Slave Narratives: A Folk History of Slavery in the United States from Interviews with Former Slaves*, Arkansas Narratives, Part 6, Kessinger Publishing, 2004.

About the Author

Sylvester Antley Clark Sr., was born on February 1, 1969, in Harlem, New York, to Garnett W. Clark and Flormae Antley, now Flormae Scott the first female Minister of Mt Calvary Baptist Church in Beaufort, South Carolina (a trailblazer). The oldest of three children, Sylvester lived with his mother, step-father and brother from age 5 until age 13 in Columbus, Ohio.

At age 13 Sylvester, his mother and brother moved to his mother's hometown in Beaufort, South Carolina with his grandparents Festus and Mary Antley and a host of uncles, aunts, and cousins, whom he now refers to as CuzBro's and CuzSis's, because their cousins, but they grew up with the bond of brothers and sisters. Sylvester was known mostly for his athleticism, but his mother always wanted him to sing. Sylvester would sing in the church choir from time to time, but he didn't feel singing was physical enough for him.

From the time Sylvester was six years old he wanted to be a professional football player and he worked hard to see that dream come to pass. Sylvester received a football scholarship from St. Paul University in 1987. After attending summer practice and making the team Sylvester left school 3 weeks into the school year. He enlisted in the US Army, came back to Beaufort and married his high school sweetheart and current wife of 34 years, Paula Doe, born in Beaufort, SC to Macon Doe and Lucille Kelson-Mullen. Paula's mother was the first woman Orthodontic lab technician in the state of South Carolina (a trailblazer). Paula has given Sylvester three wonderful sons—Sylvester Jr., Joshua, and Christopher. God has also blessed them with an amazing daughter, Angel.

Sylvester was in the 82nd Airborne Division—an elite combat division of the US Army. He went to his first combat zone nine months after arriving at his duty station in Fort Bragg, North Carolina, where he received a Bronze Star for bravery during combat. Sylvester was later released to the Fort Bragg boxing team where he was selected for the All Army Boxing team and in 1994, after winning the Army-European Championship, Sylvester was selected for the World Class Athlete Program for an opportunity to compete in the 1996 Olympics. The 24 best boxers in the Army were stationed in Fort Bragg, North Carolina and Fort Huachuca, Arizona—Sylvester was stationed in Fort Huachuca, Arizona.

Let's back track for a moment. In 1993 Sylvester gave his life to Christ in New Birth COGIC in Hanau, Germany. After this life altering experience Sylvester's boxing style changed a little bit. He was less aggressive and a little kinder to his opponents. But when he got to Fort Huachuca he felt he needed the old Sylvester back for the level of competition he had to face. This didn't work out well, because the old Sylvester didn't just want to limit himself to the ring. So, Sylvester felt he had a decision to make—which was really no decision for him. Sylvester stopped boxing and accepted his calling as a minister in 1996.

Sylvester, wife and son moved to Augusta, Georgia where Sylvester served God and studied God's Word faithfully. After much study Sylvester felt he might have acted hastily as it pertained to boxing, so he returned to the sport in 1999, winning the Georgia State Golden Gloves, then turning Pro in 2000. Sylvester boxed professionally until 2004, but he never got comfortable with it. Working two and three jobs at a time and still trying to train just wasn't working. Boxing is a sport that you have to be totally in, because your life is literally on the line.

As over the years Sylvester has learned this similarity about ministry, you have to be all in, because other people's lives are literally on the line. So Sylvester stopped boxing in 2004 and went back in the Army Reserves as a Chaplain Assistant. Sylvester has since earned his BA degree in Religion, MA in Psychology, Specialization; Sports and Peak Performance, and is currently working on his Dissertation for his PhD in Human Services.

Along with his lovely wife Paula, Sylvester has founded Universal Restoration Ministry In Action, which is dedicated to the Great Commission (spreading the Gospel to the whole world) and helping followers of Jesus Christ grow into the fullness of Christ.

Made in the USA
Columbia, SC
30 October 2023